7 STEPS TO
VIBRANT
LIVING

By
Stacy Harmer

2015

7 Steps to Vibrant Living

Copyright © 2015 by Stacy Harmer

To contact the publisher, visit
www.StacyHarmer.com

To contact the author, visit
www.StacyHarmer.com

ISBN: 978-1508944355

Printed in the United States of America

Table of Contents

Reviews

"This program is life changing. It really helps to break into baby steps the things you can do to take control of your life and feel increased peace and serenity. Stacy is a wonderful mentor and has a wealth of knowledge, resources and experience that equip her to motivate and inspire women to discover who they are and be their best selves!"

— Melanie Connell

"I had been struggling for years to put my life in order. I have felt a lot of stress and confusion as I tried to know what to do first and in what order to pursue healing in my life. I felt like I was always running around, using all my energy, and still not making any noticeable progress. I was very frustrated and worn down. This program came into my life at the perfect time for me. Looking at my life in the symbolism of a tree helped me put things in order and know where to focus my energy. One of the most powerful aspects for me was learning how to nourish my mind. I never thought that taking care of the thoughts I believed would change my whole life for the better. This program has changed my life in beautiful ways. I feel so much more whole and peaceful. What a blessing Stacy and her mentoring has been in my life."

— Christine Isom

"Stacy, I've truly loved reading your book!!! Your tips and techniques are easy to understand and are packed with an enormous amount of insight into how to live a vibrant life!!! This book is a must read for everyone. Thank you for sharing your story and experiences with all of us as we navigate our own journeys."

— Carol Carey

"In a world of negative messages and images that assault us, Stacy has provided a nurturing bag of tools that is powerful to the heart, mind, body and soul of the individual and greater community. She reaches out to those recesses of your heart that may have lain dormant, hidden, or simply forgotten and opens that tender powerful part of us that can reach out and bless others' lives. Her teaching style is approachable and applicable and can transform your life for the better, as it has mine."

- Cami Slade

"This program came into my life at exactly the right moment. I was so ready to take the steps Stacy outlined. I felt a loving bond and admiration for all the women in my group. Stacy led the group with grace and charm. I am so excited to continue on the path the program has set out so clearly for me."

- Kerry Smitheram

"Stacy is a caring, inspiring coach and mentor. Because she lives what she teaches, she has moral authority. Filling you with ideas and clarity, you are in the driver's seat and have the wheel, yet she is there to support your life's journey. I appreciate the growth I made with this program. It truly was a breakthrough process for me. Giving me tools and a plan, organizing it into a lifestyle, and making it easy to implement, it helped me to progress forward with passion and healthy systems. I became clear on what I really wanted and became a better me, wife, and mother because of it. Thank you!"

- Debbie Warner

"I first heard Stacy speak at a mom's retreat. Her smile and vibrant personality captivated me, but I felt like the few short hours I spent listening to her were not enough! That is why I am so excited about her book! This book provides insight about what it takes to live the life we were meant to live! She gives clear, concise information about how we can nourish each part of our life so that we can become the person we dream of becoming. She uses stories from her own personal life to illustrate the principles she teaches giving her reader a vision of what they can achieve."

- Lori King

"A change of life, a healthier life in body, soul and mind. How to achieve this, that's what this book is about. It starts with the author writing about the most devastating time in her life, the loss of her 5-year-old daughter after a brief illness and how she dealt with the pain and grief. Stacy gives you a view on that dark period and the seven steps she took to get rid of the darkest thoughts and head towards a vibrant life. The book is inspiring to everyone, it illustrates that everyone can achieve any goal and become whoever they want to be. A powerful book for a vibrant life…"

- Nicole Duellaert

"Stacy Harmer allows us into the private corners of her life, and then shares the strategies she employed to get out of the darkness of depression back into the light of joy. After enduring a traumatic experience, she then dedicated herself to learning and absorbing from every teacher possible to continue her healing. She willingly shares her template in this book, so we can sail through our own trials with her experience to guide us!"

- Kathleen Rockney, Nutrition Advisor
and former fibromyalgia sufferer

"Stacy Harmer is my sister by birth, my mentor and dearest friend by choice. She has walked a path few are required to walk. These experiences could have crushed her. Instead, she has triumphed; becoming the beautiful, refined, knowledgeable woman she is today. Stacy is a perpetual student - continually learning, always growing and ever willing to share what she has learned. Her wisdom, empathy and understanding bless my life on a daily basis.

"Finding balance in life is such a challenge. Stacy has lovingly and gently influenced me, helping me break through personal roadblocks and issues to become the woman I am striving to be. Her ability to connect with the "whole person" - body, heart, mind and soul - is intuitive and powerful. If you'll let them, Stacy's insights, visual anchors, and concrete suggestions will change your life."

- Collette Larsen, Business Mentor &
10 Star Diamond Director for Usana Health Sciences

"I am so grateful to have met you Stacy. What an amazing mind and heart you have. You have an incredible connection into the lives of other people. Your level of understanding and comprehension of life is astounding! I am amazed at your ability to teach, lead and inspire people. It seems as though whoever gets close to you is blessed by your wisdom and love that you have for them. I know that my life has improved since meeting you. You have caused me to live more with purpose and with passion. I am impressed with the path that you are on and I hope...I hope that more people will see what you have found. It is truly a blessing and gift that you offer to everyone that connects with you. Thank you for influencing me, which influenced my family and which assists me to influence others for good. I have risen to new heights because of your direct influence. Thank you!"

- Kirk Duncan, President 3 Key Elements

Acknowledgments

I would like to express my love and gratitude to the following people:

Olivia Grace Harmer for blessing and filling our lives with love, light, laughter, fun and excitement for five wonderful years.

My husband, Matt, who is my rock, my hero, my best friend, the love of my life and the man of my dreams. He has been faithfully by my side offering help, support, love and encouragement both over the good times and challenging times of our lives.

My children Jordan, Christian, Aubrey, Hunter, Olivia, Isabella and Gabriella for making it such a joy to be a mother. You've been a gift from God and have been a source of great joy and fulfillment in my life. Thank you for loving me and being strong through the ups and downs of life.

My wonderful son-in-law, Brian, and daughters-in-law, Katie and Lindsay. We love you as our own children and are grateful for the goodness you bring into our family and for loving our children.

My parents, Keith and Betty Larsen, and Matt's parents, John and Carolyn Harmer. We couldn't have asked for better parents and grandparents. You've been such an anchor for our family over the years. Thank you for your selfless service and Christ-like love.

My siblings and their spouses: Collette, Ric, Bob, Linda, Mike, Jenny, Sydney, Lee, Randy, Dallin, Karree, Derek, Katy, Chad, Robbi, Shawn and Jenn, and Matt's siblings and spouses: Dave, Elayne, Vivian, Mark, Chris, Rochelle, Elizabeth, Keith, Joe, Christina, Jonny, Lynnelle, Amy, Jon, Miriam, Wendy and Micah. You came to our side in our darkest hour and offered your love and support. Thank you for your friendship and example.

Our many nieces, nephews, aunts, uncles and cousins. We love you and thank you for blessing our lives.

Our many friends who have supported us on this journey. There are too many to list everyone individually, but a few that I want to mention who were by our side during this journey were Rob and Becki, Ginger, Stefany, Kelli, Becky, Angel, Kimberly, Sharlie. There are many, many others who have held our hearts and kept our family in their prayers and thoughts. We are better people because of you.

Joshua and Lindsay for encouraging me to get this book done and offering the support, guidance and structure to get this accomplished.

My Father in Heaven and Savior Jesus Christ for allowing the healing to take place in my life following some incredibly challenging experiences. Hope comes from both of them and from the infinite Atonement of Jesus Christ. It is where I have found my healing. One thing I've learned for sure is that despite our ups and downs on this mortal journey, they are always near and will never let us down as we come to them with full purpose of heart.

Introduction

I'm passionate about living a vibrant life and finding joy, now! Why? Because I know what it feels like to not have a happy, whole, healthy and vibrant life and to be stuck in a pit of darkness. It has become my mission to share and teach to others the tools that I have discovered during my own healing journey through the sadness and grief of unexpectedly losing a beloved daughter. My journey took me further down as I spiraled into a deep clinical depression a couple of years after her passing. After years of learning and healing, I feel like I have discovered a formula to help others find joy, now, despite the challenges they may be facing. I describe my experience as going from the Pit to the Promised Land.

Every healing journey is personal, but as my path unfolded before me, the journey I went on was one of discovery, trial and error, progress and growth. As I began changing and healing personally, I began to teach small groups of women these principles, and I would hear great results from those with whom I shared these ideas. Then I began teaching larger groups, workshops and seminars to both men and women. My desire in writing this book is to reach more people and offer them the formula, tools and steps I discovered on my journey of healing.

This book is for the person who wants to move from hitting barriers to having breakthroughs in their life. It is meant for people who are looking to find more joy and meaning in their experiences. It is for the individual who has struggles with depression or discouragement. It is for the entrepreneur who can't seem to get their ideas off of the ground. The first step to being successful in business is to become a healthy, whole person in body, heart, mind and spirit. It is for the individual who may be suffering from grief and loss of a loved one. Finally, it is for people who desire to fulfill the measure of their creation.

I believe we are meant to share the lessons we learn in life. If not, what is the purpose behind them? We may grow from our experiences, but how much greater is it if we can help and assist others to grow, as well? In sharing, we gain purpose and meaning to our experiences, trials, and challenges. I sincerely hope you will find nuggets of insight and value for your own life throughout the pages of this book. I do share some of my very personal journey. One of my heroes, Mahatma Gandhi said, "My life is my message." And so it is with me. Many of the experiences in my life are things I wouldn't have hoped or wished for, but when we look to the Light and Source of all, we can find the goodness in everything. I am grateful to my Divine Source for the strength and guidance I've been given throughout this journey. All of the tools I share in this book I have studied, learned, and implemented firsthand. I'm not always perfect, but as you'll hear several times throughout the book, *life is about progress, not perfection.*

Stacy Harmer

Chapter 1

Why a Vibrant and Joyful Life?

W hy live a Vibrant and Joyful Life? Of course we are meant to have a happy, healthy life. We are created to have joy. But, first I want to create a vision of why this is important. I'll start off by posing a question. What do salt and light have in common? In my core book, we are instructed to be the "salt of the earth" and also be a "light upon a hill." Both salt and light influence their surroundings in a positive way. Salt enhances the flavor of anything it touches. Light illuminates any object it comes in contact with. We are meant to be leaders and influence for good all that we touch or are involved with. Our lives are meant to have purpose and meaning. We are not meant to simply take up space but to fulfill all that we are meant to become.

One of my favorite books is *The Chosen* by Chaim Potok. It is a story about two Jewish boys, Rueven and Danny, the friendship they develop, and the relationships they both have with their fathers. Reuven's father is very wise and shares with his son why he works tirelessly on the causes that mean so much to him even though his health suffers because of it.

"Human beings do not live forever. We live less than the time it takes to blink an eye, if we measure our lives against eternity... I learned a long time ago, that a blink of an eye in itself is nothing. But the eye that blinks, that is something. A span of life is nothing. But the man who lives that span, he is something. He can fill that tiny span with meaning, so its quality is immeasurable though its quantity may be insignificant... A man must fill his life with meaning; meaning is not automatically given to life. It is hard work to fill one's life with meaning... Merely to live, merely to exist – what sense is there to it? A fly also lives."

The whole reason to have a vibrant life is to live a life of meaning and purpose and to be able to change the world in some way for the better.

This is where we find a great deal of joy and zest for life. As we begin to really discover our strengths, natural gifts, talents and personality and even acknowledge our difficult and challenging life experiences, our purpose begins to unfold.

It is inevitable that we'll have challenges and stumbling blocks along the way, but the key is to be able to look at the stumbling blocks and turn them into stepping-stones. The quicker we can identify our blocks and be proactive in using them to continue moving forward, the quicker we are able to continue on our journey of progression.

Five Areas of Alignment
Ripples of Influence

In order to have a greater outreach for good and personal peace in our lives, I have found that it is crucial to keep our lives in alignment. When we are out of balance or out of alignment, life becomes a struggle. One of my greatest desires is to have peace. I also desire to do as much good as I possibly can, but I've learned through trial and error that I must keep myself in check. It is easy to lose focus or get off on a tangent and then realize we have drifted far from our original course. It is important to stay aligned with our priorities if we are meant to have peace in our lives. I've developed an analogy in my life to keep myself constantly in check as I move down any particular path. I call it Ripples of Influence.

Source

To illustrate this principle, imagine tossing a rock into a pond. What happens to the water? It creates ripples, right? Well, the larger the rock, the larger the ripples. The rock represents our Source or Higher Power. It is because of that rock that the ripples are created in the first place. So, in our personal lives, if we can keep our lives in alignment with our Higher Power or Source, we will feel at peace and know that we are on the right course, which aligns with our values and priorities. Connecting with our Higher Power can be done in many ways. Some possibilities are prayer, meditation, journaling, reading scriptures, being in nature, etc. I'll go into much more detail in an upcoming chapter on how to Nourish our Spirit and more fully connect with our Higher Power.

Self

The first ripple out represents Self. This is not meant in a selfish way, but it is difficult to give out when we ourselves are depleted. You must fill your own bucket before you can share with another. When riding on an airplane, they tell you in case of an emergency to grab your own oxygen mask and secure it before assisting children with theirs. This is a concept that is difficult for a lot of mothers and women. It is so easy to put the needs of our children, spouse, neighborhood, and school before making sure that our needs are met to keep us healthy and strong.

This book basically describes how to meet our personal needs in order to grow beautifully and to be able to really produce fruit and make a difference in the lives of others. It boils down to nourishing our bodies, hearts, minds and souls on a daily basis. This book will describe in much more detail how to do this, but nourishing our bodies has to do with getting proper nutrition, sleep, exercise, adequate hydration, etc. To nourish our heart means we focus on expanding and opening up our heart. We can do this not only by acts of service and kindness but also by releasing the negative emotions that we may be holding on to and replacing them with peace, joy, forgiveness, love and gratitude. To nourish our mind means to learn, study and grow. It also means using our minds to create the lives we desire by focusing our thoughts, creating affirmations, and using a dream board among other things. Lastly, we need to nourish our spirits on a daily basis. This is connecting to your Higher Power in a meaningful way, which may include prayer, meditation, reading scriptures, journaling, being in nature and any other practice that brings you closer to your Higher Power.

Spouse

After the ripple of Self comes the next ripple, which is your Spouse, if you are married. We have high hopes and dreams when we marry our sweethearts, but with the demands of life, children, work, school or finances that begin to consume our lives, our spouses often get put on the back burner. This may work in the beginning, but eventually not keeping this in alignment will result in dissatisfaction and frustration. The 50% divorce rate in this country shows just how often marriages fall apart, and many of those who choose to remain married are dissatisfied. If you are going to spend your time and life with another individual, they, and you, deserve to make this a priority in your life. No one likes to simply exist or endure. That would drain all the energy and vitality out of life.

Date nights have become a weekly ritual in my relationship with my spouse. Even though we may have many and varied demands and responsibilities, we try to set aside a night a week for just us as a couple. Another idea that has helped us is that we have created a "Love Menu." We talked and then shared a list of items that would make us each feel loved. It is really enlightening to hear from your spouse the things that they would like or need to feel loved. Sometimes we just don't get it, and we have different love languages, and the love that we may desire to give just doesn't get through to the other person. Simply having a conversation about things that would make each other feel loved is a wonderful resource.

Children

The next ripple out is for the children in your family. Nurturing this relationship is so important in our families. It is easy to get caught up with the busyness and demands of life and not give this area the attention that it deserves. Time is fleeting, and our children grow up before we know it. We never know when something could happen where these precious children may be taken. I remember the morning that my Olivia passed away so suddenly and unexpectedly, my heart broke into a million pieces. The thought that I wouldn't have more time with her on this earth was devastating to me. I had tried to be the best mom I could, but I was also busy with many demands on my time. Oh how I wished I could go back and take advantage of every moment I had with my daughter.

One thing we've implemented in our home over the years is individual date nights with our children. When our son Christian was in college, he shared a paper he had written about his favorite memories of childhood. The one thing that he loved the most was to have individual date nights with Mom or Dad. He said that this really made him feel special and important. With these relationships, it takes planning and calendaring, or they just don't happen. Having a weekly family council has been a staple in our home. Simply to pull out our calendars for the week and schedule

13

what is going on so everyone is on the same page is very helpful. Once again, if it isn't on the calendar, it likely won't happen.

Community and World

The next ripple is to influence our extended family, community and world. Our outreach can go out as far and wide as we are willing to put ourselves. As I mentioned earlier, we are meant to be a light to the world, and share that light with others. There was a time in my life when I studied many great leaders and statesman from throughout the world. These were individuals who truly made an impact in the world for the better. One such individual I studied was Mahatma Gandhi. He said, "Be the change you want to see in the world." He lived his life this way.

Once we identify our gifts, talents and passions, then it really is incumbent upon us to share those with the people we love and spread it as far and wide as we desire. A great leader is one who sees the world the way it is, sees it the way it should be, and then has the courage to step up and stand in the middle to bridge the gap and say "Here am I. I can help bridge that gap." I think of people such as Martin Luther, Gandhi, Martin Luther King, Jr., Winston Churchill, Joan of Arc, Florence Nightingale, Mother Teresa, Abraham Lincoln, George Washington and so many others.

As long as our lives are aligned, we will feel peace and use our talents and strengths for good. I have seen others who want to change the world for the better but then have neglected their most important relationships with spouse and children, and then resentment and discontent build up. No matter how much good we do in this world, if our primary relationships are broken, we won't be as effective as we could be or find the meaning and fulfillment that we desire.

Supportive Activities:

1. One of the best tools we have is our own inner guidance. As we become more self aware, we can always find answers within to any given problem. In the left column, list 3 stumbling blocks you have in your life right now. If you could master them, your life would go more smoothly. Now, in the right column, turn those stumbling blocks into stepping-stones. Make a list of 3 things you could do to turn each stumbling block into a stepping-stone.

STUMBLING BLOCKS	STEPPING STONES

2. Take a look at the Five Ripple Areas in your life and evaluate how you are doing in each of these areas. Are they aligned? Do they match with your values? If not, create some action items in each area to give them proper attention and alignment. Remember the Ripple Effect. Each area represents a ripple, and in order to have further outreach, we must have our inner areas and circles in order.

    1. Source

    2. Self

    3. Spouse

    4. Children

    5. Community and World

Chapter 2

My Story - Adopting Olivia

We had been blessed with four wonderful children, and I loved being a mom and truly found great satisfaction in raising and playing with my children. But, something seemed to be missing. I really felt like our family wasn't complete and deeply wanted another child. My husband didn't share my same feelings or desires. This issue always seemed to creep up in our relationship, and we couldn't seem to come to an agreement.

I'm a deeply spiritual person. One morning, as I was pouring my heart out to my Father in Heaven in prayer trying to understand His will as well as expressing my desire for another child, I had a simple but profound experience. As I was reading in my scriptures in the Book of Esther, I had the clear and distinct impression that we had another daughter, but she wouldn't come to us in the traditional way. I felt impressed that we would adopt her and she would be a different nationality. Like Esther, she would be beautiful, chosen by the King, and be instrumental in saving her people. I wasn't sure what all this meant, but since I'm an intuitive and spiritual person, I trusted that this would be the case.

I wondered how my husband would react to this. We both knew that we had been abundantly blessed, and he had a good heart. When I approached him about adopting, his heart was open to that possibility because he felt like that was something we could do to also bless a child that needed a home.

It wasn't that quick or easy, but suffice it to say, we did get the process started. Participating in an international adoption is quite an ordeal, and it was for us as well. It involved months and months of paperwork, fingerprinting, interviews, patience, etc. During this waiting time, I had another profound experience as I was up early one morning and reading my scriptures. I was reading about an analogy of an Olive Tree, and that the Lord of the Vineyard grafted different branches into trees that needed to be strengthened. The very clear and distinct thought came to me that our daughter would play that role in our family. She would be grafted into our family to strengthen my family tree. After this experience, I knew immediately what I wanted to name her - Olivia Grace. Olivia was for the Olive Tree and Grace was a blessing from God, and I knew that was what she would be. When I shared this with my husband, he was open and willing to name her this.

The day finally arrived when we received our referral. She was a darling little Korean girl with tons of hair. We then were able to meet and bring her home two months later. She was escorted to Seattle where we first met her and then brought her home to our family. This was in the year 2000, before all of the airport security, so we were able to meet her at the gate when she was carried off the plane. I can't begin to even describe the absolute joy, tears and happiness I felt as this tiny little four-month-old baby was placed in my arms. She was only 13 lbs., and felt like a newborn baby to me.

I admit that the feeling I had when she was placed in my arms was absolutely no different than when each of my children that I had given birth to were placed in my arms. There was an absolute instant bond and outflow of love that was incredible to experience. She was so calm and content and had gobs and gobs of hair. I couldn't contain my tears, and knew that God had blessed us with a sweet angel baby who would bless our lives immensely.

It was so much fun to then fly home to Salt Lake City for the rest of our family to meet her. When we arrived at the airport, we probably had forty people gathered at the gate waiting to welcome us home. Our four blond children, ages five to thirteen, were ecstatic and were jumping for joy, each eager to hold their new precious sister. This was just days before Christmas, so as you can imagine, our home was overflowing with love and joy this Christmas for our long-anticipated arrival.

I describe the years that Olivia graced our family as literally "Heaven on Earth." Little did we know that our time would be limited with this angel, but she became the center of our family and existence. We all loved her so much, and she had each of our hearts tied around her little finger. She honestly could get anything she wanted because she had that much charm and influence over us! During this time, I also began homeschooling my other children. This was quite an adventure, and one that we loved. We moved to San Diego, and that was the greatest place to homeschool a family with all of the wonderful museums, beaches and activities that we could participate in, not to mention the thriving community that we participated in with many of our very closest friends. Olivia was surrounded by her siblings, family and friends who adored her every moment of her life.

One afternoon in 2005, I was mentoring a group of women in my home. We were studying the classics and would read, write and discuss different books and themes. We met at my home every week. As usually happens with a group of women who share in that type of setting, we all grew to love and support each other. I remember thinking about each of these women. They had all gone through some significant challenges in their lives. Among some of the challenges were divorce, serious illness, difficult children, raising siblings because a mother had passed away, a serious accident that had left one bedridden for many years, etc. I deeply loved and appreciated each of them.

After they all left my home one afternoon and after hearing of some of their challenges, I remember going upstairs to my bedroom and leaning against my door. I said a little prayer in my heart to my Father in Heaven. I told Him that I wanted to assist Him in helping others who were struggling and going through hard times. My life had its ups and downs but had been relatively a piece of cake compared to others. I said I would be His servant, but I did give one caveat. That was that I just didn't want to go through ANY of their hard stuff. I would devote my life to love and serve others, but only if I didn't have to go through the hard stuff myself. I really didn't think much more of that little prayer until around two weeks later when my life was completely shattered and would change its course forever.

Losing Olivia

Never in a million years would I have dreamed we would soon go through the heart-wrenching experience awaiting us. Olivia was our everything. She was the center of our family. It was so fun to see the children all wanting to be her "best buddy" because that was a coveted position. Everyone wanted to be her favorite! It was almost like she was the glue that held us together. So, to find her that morning was almost more than we could bear. She passed away unexpectedly in her sleep following a brief illness. I won't go into all the details here, but the shock and trauma of that event still can instantly stir up painful feelings of grief that cut to the core.

Much healing has taken place, but I still do occasionally have my difficult days. We couldn't imagine our lives without our little angel. How could we possibly carry on? It was five years to the day that she was first placed in our arms that we had to lay her body to rest. We immediately felt the outpouring of love and support. We had never been so surrounded by so much love. It was palpable. Between receiving loving notes, gifts, flowers, acts of kindness, listening ears, food, etc., our hearts were being held in a safe and protected place.

I had been given some sweet spiritual assurances that all would be well. I knew that Olivia was in a beautiful place welcomed by all of our loved ones. I turned to my Savior and personal Source, Jesus Christ, like I never had before. It has always been my belief that there was an Atonement, and He was the only one that could carry our pain and burden. As I began pouring my heart out to Him and pleading for help, beautiful things began happening in my life. I was blessed with a great amount of light and understanding. I would often wake up very early in the morning and spend hours on my knees in prayer, meditation and journaling. All these things strengthened me, and I tried to hold on to them with all of my might.

But, there was one little problem. Our minds are powerful forces and our thoughts can take us to places that can bring us down pretty quickly if we allow them to. When I would start dwelling on "if only..." or "what if...", I would begin spiraling downward, feeling like a failure as a mother and to God and my family. It hurt my heart so deeply that I didn't know if I could go on. Then I would have the sweet spiritual assurances, and I would hold on.

Not long after Olivia's passing, we moved back to Utah, changed jobs and tried to rebuild our lives. I had come to understand the power of Light, but there is opposition in all things, and that also brought great amounts of darkness, as I would go into the negative thinking. After a couple of years, my body, mind, spirit and heart simply broke down, and I spiraled into a clinical depression. Those are days that I don't like to dwell on because it was a painful time in all of our lives. Not only had we lost our beloved Olivia, but now my family was losing me as well.

Lucky for me, I was surrounded by people who loved me and were very concerned about what was happening to me. My husband stepped in after months of painfully watching me spiral downward. He got me the medical help that was necessary to put me on the track of recovery. I will forever be grateful to him as my hero who literally saved my life.

I don't like to dwell on the dark path that I walked and the hopelessness and despair that engulfed me. I won't go into the details of those experiences because that is not where I want to focus my energy. I know that whatever we focus on grows and expands. I learned from hard experience that, as I would focus on my pain, grief, and feelings of failure with the thoughts of "if only..." and "what if...," my darkness would grow until I was trapped with no way out.

I was lucky enough to receive some help, intervention and medical attention during this time in my life to get back on my feet, but I had a long healing journey ahead of me.

Chapter 3

The Healing Journey

I would wake up in the mornings and begin writing. I was reading the book *The Artist's Way* by Julia Cameron where she described Morning Notes. They are a way to declutter your mind and thoughts, and put them down on paper. Through this process of getting the whirling thoughts down on paper and clearing your head, you open up space to allow your creativity, insight and inspiration to flow. As I would engage in this process nearly every morning before anyone else woke up, I would pour my heart out to my Higher Power to guide and help me know the steps I needed to take to heal my life.

The Tree Analogy

Roots

One morning, thoughts and ideas started pouring into my head as I was doing my Morning Notes. I started sketching out a tree with the roots running deeply into the soil. Four distinct roots emerged. We are multi-dimensional beings, and the four roots seemed to represent our body, heart, mind and soul. Just as a tree needs to get constant nourishment from the rich soil and water reaching its roots to sustain growth, we need to nourish our body, heart, mind and soul on a daily basis as well. It is something now that I put on my daily "To Do" list and strive to nourish those roots daily by incorporating specific practices in each area.

Trunk

The trunk of a tree represents form or the structure – holding things together and helping to sustain the growth. In our personal lives, we also need structure, forms or systems to keep our lives running smoothly. I know as a busy mother and also a Health Coach, I need systems in all areas of my life in order to run more smoothly. S.Y.S.T.E.M stands for Save Your Self Time Energy and Money. Once we identify the roles that we have in our lives and implement systems, we can feel more on top of our lives and can find greater balance to our demands as well as streamline many of the daily and weekly tasks we do.

Branches

The branches of the tree represent finding our Purpose and Passion. To me, this is really the fun part of life! When we are living our purpose and passion, everything is brighter and more vibrant and we find joy in all that we do. We find our purpose by utilizing our strengths, abilities and talents. Often it is the difficult things in life that point us to the direction where we are meant to be of most service. When we find our voice, a new zest for life and energy just flows!

Fruit

Finally, the fruit of the tree represents sharing our unique gifts with others. Often times if a fruit tree is not producing fruit, it is because it is not receiving the proper nourishment to the roots. It may be diseased or sick. But, if a healthy tree is producing fruit, if that fruit is not harvested and picked from the tree, what happens? We've all seen trees with ripened fruit that has fallen to the ground without harvesting, and consequently the fruit begins to rot and make a mess! In our own lives, the fruit represents our gifts and talents. If we are not then sharing these gifts to fulfill our purpose and passion, those gifts and talents lie dormant and we begin making a mess in our own lives.

It is only by giving and receiving that the flow of life occurs. Why is the Dead Sea called the Dead Sea? Because there is no outflow. The air in a room without ventilation becomes stale. A soaking wet sponge in a sink without the release of the water soon becomes stinky.

All of these images began flowing into my mind, and I realized the importance of sharing the fruit in our lives if our personal trees were producing fruit. At the time I was discovering all of this and creating the analogy on paper, I personally was not producing fruit in my own life. I needed a great deal of daily nourishment to my roots - my body, heart, mind and soul - on a regular basis. That is where I began focusing.

In the law of the harvest, there is a gestational period where time must pass before the fruit is produced. I learned that I needed to be patient during this time in my life. As much as I wanted to be out there making an impact or difference in the lives of others, I knew that my focus at this time had to be getting myself healthy and whole again. That is when I started learning and implementing the practices of nourishing my body, heart, mind and soul on a regular basis.

As we follow this pattern, something beautiful and amazing happens in our lives. Our roots grow deeper. We set up Systems to help our lives run more smoothly. We begin discovering our Purpose and Passion and then we naturally share our gifts, talents and fruit.

Supportive Activity:

Evaluate how you are doing in the following 7 areas in your life. Rate yourself from 1-10. In order to make changes in our lives, it is important to know where we are starting. Be honest with yourself. This will be a good starting place as you read the rest of the book. Each area presented below will be discussed in detail along with a number of tools and activities to help you reach a 10 in each area of your life.

Body - Healthy eating, exercise, sleep, etc. 1-10:

Heart - Positive feelings of peace, love, joy, forgiveness and gratitude, giving and serving in your life. 1-10:

Mind - Reading uplifting and inspiring materials, having positive thoughts, affirmations, focus, intention, etc. 1-10:

Soul - Connecting to your Divine Source through prayer, studying scriptures, journaling, meditation, walking in nature, etc. 1-10:

Systems and Structure - Having clear systems and routines in your daily life to help your life run more smoothly. 1-10:

Discovering Your Purpose and Passion - Knowing what your strengths, abilities, talents, and passions are. 1-10:

Sharing Your Gifts - Actively sharing your gifts and talents with family, friends or community to bless the lives of others and make a positive impact in the world. 1-10:

Chapter 4

Roots: Nourishing The Body

Our body is the first root that we need to address. It is a gift that we must protect and care for the best way possible. If we were given one car to last us our lifetime, how would we care for it? I know that I would be proactive in making sure that I did all of the scheduled maintenance, get the oil changed regularly and feed it the best fuel possible. Our bodies are really no different. We get one body to last our lifetime, and how we care for it or what we put into our bodies does make a huge difference in our quality of life.

As with everything I'm going to share in this book, I've experienced this personally. The foods we eat are meant to nourish our bodies physically, and we call them Secondary Foods. We get our primary fulfillment in other areas of our life such as Spirituality, Relationships, Physical Activity and Careers or Personal Mission. If there are holes in those areas of our lives, we are often likely to turn to food to fill those holes and may develop unhealthy habits.

When dealing with the immense amount of emotions related to my daughter's passing and then the depression that followed, I turned to food as a way to smother the pain. I suppose I am grateful that I turned to food rather than something more destructive, but I definitely developed some addictive behaviors, patterns and habits, not to mention adding an additional 25 lbs. to my body. I felt as if I was in a vicious cycle and could hardly make it through the day without my "chocolate fix!" I began to realize I had a problem, and my willpower didn't seem strong enough to fix it on its own.

Then one day in February, my husband came home from work and said that some of his coworkers had decided to give up alcohol for Lent. Lent is a sacred religious observance by some Christian denominations in preparation for the celebration of Easter. Often people give up something or participate in some kind of fast. I had never observed Lent before, but

I liked the idea of deliberately spiritually preparing myself for Easter. Through my healing, I had come to know my Higher Power more than I ever thought possible. I attribute my healing to Him and feel immense gratitude for that! I loved the idea of sacrificing something for Him in preparation for this season of deep meaning. As I thought about it, I knew that I needed to give up chocolate and desserts for Lent. This would truly be a sacrifice for me, and I knew that He knew that! In return, I asked for some pretty amazing spiritual gifts. My husband also decided to give up ice cream and chocolate along with me.

All I can say is that period of time changed my life!! This higher purpose was able to trump my own willpower. I admit I was not 100% perfect at it but probably 98%, and that was far more than I had ever done on my own. Then the spiritual gifts that I had prayed for came flowing into my life so abundantly, that I was pretty blown away. He never disappoints! So this little experiment taught me personally how our spiritual awareness is linked to what we take into our bodies. I then started really examining other ways I was eating. I began cutting out refined flours and sugars and replacing them with whole grains and natural sweeteners. I felt like I was on a mission to transform not only the way I eat but how I fed my family.

I personally now strive for a relatively high raw diet and feed my children MANY more whole and raw foods while drastically cutting out the highly processed and refined foods. Oh, the ENERGY and CLARITY that comes with feeding our bodies in healthy ways is fabulous! Have you ever felt the slow, sluggishness and mental confusion that comes with overeating refined sugars, flours and overly processed foods? It's worth it to experiment to make a shift.

We all need food and nourishment to survive, but as we properly take care of our bodies, then we can also thrive in our personal lives. Each of the subject areas below could have their own complete book or course of study, but for the sake of all the content that is included in this book, I'll just touch on them briefly.

I like to use acronyms to help me remember things. I tend to have lots of thoughts running through my brain, so if I can simplify to remember things, it is helpful. The acronym I came up with for nourishing our body is P.L.E.A.S.E. As you think of this word and the explanation I share below, you'll be armed with accessible information to keep your body in tip top shape.

P.L.E.A.S.E.   P - Proper Supplementation

Even with the best diet, it is difficult to obtain all that we need from foods in this day and age. It is important to get cellular nutrition. The medical literature is beginning to address what is at the root of over 70 chronic degenerative diseases. That is oxidative stress. That is when an oxygen-charged molecule produces a free radical. Free radicals damage cells, and anti-oxidants neutralize the free radical. We can get antioxidants in our fruits and vegetables, but given the amount of toxicity in our environments, food and lives, that alone isn't enough.

For optimal health, we need to supplement our diets with high quality products. The challenge is that you can't always trust the labels on supplements because the nutritional industry is an unregulated industry. It is important that you use pharmaceutical grade supplements and the best quality to ensure that you are actually getting what the label says you are getting in the appropriate amounts for your body. It is worth doing your research on the quality of supplements you are using.

One great resource is Lyle MacWilliam's *Comparative Guide to Nutritional Supplements*. This is an independent research company that compares over 1600 different nutritional supplements and gives each one of them a rating. You don't want to be wasting your money on expensive urine, but you do want to be arming your cells with the best quality nutrients and protection you can. That is why it is worth taking the time to do your research. Remember, you have just one body!

P.L.E.A.S.E.   L - Low Glycemic,
Whole and Raw Foods

There is much talk in the nutrition field about carbohydrates. Our bodies need carbohydrates for the glucose they provide for fuel. But there is a paradox here. Not only is the sugar found in carbohydrates necessary for our bodies to function properly - especially our brains - but it can also be very addictive. Some research even suggests that it is more addictive in how the brain functions than cocaine.

The glycemic index is a numerical system that rates how fast carbohydrates break down into glucose and enter the blood stream. Low glycemic foods are slowly digested and absorbed, and there is only a gentle rise in blood sugar and insulin levels. Lowering insulin levels is not only a key factor in weight loss but the secret to long-term health. But the problem with the Standard American Diet (SAD diet) is that it is full of hidden sugars and highly processed foods.

It is not only sugars such as sucrose, fructose and glucose that spike the blood sugar, but we have discovered now that any refined and highly processed foods have a high glycemic index and spike the blood sugar. For example, white bread and white flour spikes our blood sugar faster than eating spoonfuls of white sugar right out of the sugar bowl. There are several factors that influence the glycemic index. Some of these are: whole foods, fiber content, the type of sugar and how the foods are produced.

The chart on the next page will give you some idea of the glycemic index of foods.

Whole Foods

We hear a lot about whole foods, but do you know why it is important to eat them?

We live in a society where there is so much processed food that it may be confusing for some to even know what a whole food is. Quite simply, it is a food that is in its natural state. You are getting the food intact with all of the vitamins, minerals and fiber to boot. Our supermarkets look much different than they did a century ago. Rather than an abundance of food in its natural and whole state, processed food has become the norm. Supermarkets are filled with boxes of overly processed and refined foods that have been stripped of their essential nutrients. The consumer has developed a taste for the processed foods that are filled with sugars, colors, flavors and preservatives, which can be very addicting.

There are so many health benefits to eating a whole-foods diet. Many studies suggest that individuals whose diets are primarily whole foods-

Glycemic Index of Some Common Foods*

High Glycemic Index Foods (GI > 85)

Cream of Wheat	Cornmeal	English muffin	Sport drinks
Shredded Wheat	Croissant, doughnut	Mashed potatoes	Soft drinks
Total Cereal	Rice cakes	Carrots	Hard candy
Crispix Cereal	Pop-tarts	Watermelon	Jelly beans
Corn Flakes, Rice	Angel food cake	Raisins	Syrups or sucrose
Krispies, Bubbles	White bread or bagel	Pretzels	Glucose, maltose
Cheerios	Soda crackers	Couscous	Molasses
Corn Chex cereal	Corn chips	Gnocchi	Fruit Roll-Ups
Grape-Nuts	Waffles, pancakes	Vanilla Wafers	Dates

Moderate Glycemic Index Foods (GI = 60-85)

100% Whole wheat bread	Brown or wild rice	Popcorn	Grapes
Rye kernel bread	Cracked barley	Sponge cake	Grapefruit juice
7-grain bread	White rice (long grain)	Linguine, durum	Orange (whole or juice)
Pita bread, white	Buckwheat	Sweet corn	Fruit cocktail
Oat bran cereal	Basmati rice	Oat bran	Mango or papaya
Bran Chex cereal	Wheat, cooked	Oatmeal	Kiwi fruit
Special K cereal	Bulgar	Marmalade or honey	Cranberry juice
All-Bran cereal	Parboiled rice	Ice cream, low-fat	
		Sweet potato	

Low Glycemic Index Foods (GI < 60)

Barley kernel bread	Fettuccini, egg	Beans (all types)	Apples (whole or juice)
Wheat kernels	Apricots (dried)	Peaches or pears (fresh)	Power bar
Tomato soup	Rice bran	Fructose	Oat bran bread
Cherries, plums	Soy milk or drink	Hummus	Lentils
Milk (whole or nonfat)	Dried peas	Peanuts	Grapefruit
Yogurt (all types)	Banana		Peanut M&Ms
	Barley		

*White bread (50 g) was used as the reference food.

From www.dietdatabase.com

- vegetables, fruits and whole grains - also have lower risks of cardiovascular disease, some types of cancer and Type 2 Diabetes. It not only affects the health of the body, but it affects the mental, emotional and spiritual state of an individual as well.

Raw Foods

I became passionate about Raw Foods when I started experimenting with eating a high raw diet as well as getting trained as a Raw Food Chef. I started exploring all of the possibilities with creating wonderful dishes that were raw and my taste buds were doing back flips with what I discovered. You don't need to give up on flavor, variety and texture when you eat raw, but you are opening up your world to so many more possibilities. Also, I was feeling so great with increased energy and vitality. I was not finding myself in the sluggish food comas from overeating processed foods. Why eat a high raw diet? Well there are many benefits. Some of these are:

1. A raw diet is cleansing. Our bodies are constantly cleaning out toxins and repairing tissues, but when we overload our bodies with processed foods, toxins from our food and environment, our bodies can't keep up. Toxins build up, we weaken our bodies and our health declines. Our bodies become sluggish and more vulnerable and susceptible to disease, we feel tired and our brain feels foggy, and we gain weight. When we eat clean, natural and raw foods, we have more energy and feel more alive and vibrant.

2. You'll be more hydrated. Many people don't drink adequate amounts of water and are dehydrated without even realizing it. Raw foods have more water content than cooked foods. Hydration helps our kidneys function better and improves our skin and mental focus.

3. You'll have fewer cravings. When we are nutritionally deficient, we seem to constantly snack but never get the nutrients our body is craving. When we are eating nutrient-rich raw foods, our bodies are satisfied, we don't have constant food cravings, and we feel satisfied.

4. Your immune system will be stronger. Raw foods have high amounts of vitamins and minerals that have strong antioxidant, immune-enhancing, anti-inflammatory and anti-cancer properties.

5. You will lose weight. When eating a lower calorie, fiber-rich diet, it is inevitable that you will shed extra pounds. Adding more raw foods and eliminating the processed and empty-calorie foods will help you lose that unwanted weight much quicker than you thought possible!

6. You'll slow the aging process. When we flood our bodies daily with nutrients that keep our organs running properly, we get more energy, mental clarity, hormonal balance, and fewer wrinkles. We've armed ourselves against high blood pressure, heart disease and high cholesterol.

P.L.E.A.S.E. E - Exercise

Find an exercise that you love!! If you enjoy doing it, then you will be more likely to follow through. It is important to get cardiovascular, flexibility and weight training exercise in for optimal physical well being. Some of my favorite types of exercise are Yoga, Zumba, biking and walking. I love morning nature walks with a friend because that is a great way to build friendships as well as allow an emotional release as you converse and provide a listening ear for each other. I've never been much of a runner, but I recently signed up to run my first half marathon and now have a training schedule. I was looking for somewhat of a challenge to push myself physically, so I'm going to give it a try.

Some of the many health benefits of exercising are:

1. Exercise improves your state of mind. If you are looking for something to help with mood swings, depression or anxiety, then look no further! Exercise stimulates endorphins, which help in all these areas as well as help enhance that happy feeling!

2. Exercise helps control your weight. You burn calories during exercise, which gives you the added boost in weight loss as well as getting the body you want and feeling great. A regular fitness routine will not only help you obtain the body you desire, but will also make you feel stronger and more confident.

3. Exercise helps regulate hormones. By regularly exercising, you release unwanted toxins from your body. With a reduced toxic load, your hormones can work more efficiently which will result in fewer mood swings.

4. Exercise decreases the risk of disease and other health conditions. Exercise has been proven to improve cardiovascular health, boost circulation, reduce "bad" cholesterol and balance blood sugar, which results in decreased food cravings.

5. Exercise improves the quality of sleep. Studies show flooding your body with more oxygen and releasing toxicity as you sweat improves the quality of sleep.

6. Exercise promotes energy. Although you may feel tired after a good workout, regular exercise boosts your energy. You are delivering more oxygen to your tissues, which results in more energy as the oxygen flows through your veins. By increasing oxygen levels in your body, you also improve digestion and overall well being.

P.L.E.A.S.E. A - Adequate Hydration

Water is the key to life on this planet, and our bodies are in desperate need of it. Adequate water improves metabolism, decreases blood pressure, and keeps a good flow going within our bodies. Inadequate hydration can impair the immune system and causes sluggish mental processing. The average adult human body is made up of approximately 60% water. A quick way to figure how much to drink daily is to take half your body weight in pounds, then drink that much in ounces (140 lbs; 70 ounces). There are many benefits to doing this, but a few are:

1. Aids in eliminating waste and toxins from your body. It improves bowel movement because of hydration and it also aids the kidneys in eliminating toxins through the urine. Also, adequate hydration aids in preventing kidney stones.

2. Makes skin look younger. Dehydration makes your skin look more wrinkled and dry, and your skin is improved by keeping it properly hydrated.

3. Maintains a balance of bodily fluids. In addition to keeping our bodies hydrated, there is some very compelling research about the effect that words have on water and how that may affect our bodies as well. There is a wonderful book, *The Hidden Messages of Water*, by Masaru Emoto. In amazing photographs, he demonstrates how different types of crystals formed in containers of water when different words were said to them. Negative words produced deformed and random crystals, while positive words produced beautifully formed crystals. It is more evidence of how our thoughts and words really do affect our health. Since our bodies are over 50% water, we should be very mindful of the words spoken and how they may affect the health of our bodies.

P.L.E.A.S.E. S - Sleep

It is imperative to our health that we get adequate rest. This is the time our body needs to rejuvenate and repair. It is recommended that adults get 7-8 hours of sleep a day. When we don't get the rest our bodies need, we become tired, irritable, have problems with concentration and memory and are unable to tolerate stress well. After I lost Olivia, I couldn't sleep. I went for two years with very little sleep. Boy, did that wreak havoc with my body and brain chemistry. I certainly paid the price for it.

P.L.E.A.S.E. E - Energy

When you put these principles into practice, you'll have ENERGY!

Remember: P L E A S E
P – Proper Supplementation
L – Low Glycemic, Whole and Raw Foods
E – Exercise
A – Adequate Hydration
S – Sleep
E – Equals ENERGY!!!!

Supportive Activity to Nourish Your Body:

What 3 things can you eliminate from your diet to be healthier? What 3 things can you add to your diet to be healthier?

Eliminate from My Diet   **Add to My Diet**

Chapter 5

Roots: Nourishing Your Heart

Our hearts are beautiful and tender things! They are where our emotions are stored. They are meant to be soft and open. But depending on our life experiences, we tend to bandage up our hearts or create walls. We don't consciously do this, but we may have been hurt deeply and want to protect our hearts, so we put up barriers.

Each of us needs to do what it takes to peel back the layers of protection on our hearts so they can be more open and soft. When we have an open and loving heart, we are able to connect deeply with others, which helps create meaningful and loving relationships.

I often pray for an open, loving, contrite and even broken heart because I know what that feels like. It allows me to be more compassionate to others and feel the pain and joy that others are going through. I also know what it feels like to have a closed and hardened heart, and I don't like to live in that place.

The challenge is, we are all mortals and experience a wide degree of emotions - fear, frustration, anger, sadness, grief, jealousy, etc., but we don't want to hold on to those emotions. When we stuff our emotions deep within our hearts, they are still alive and festering. One of my favorite books on this subject is *Feelings Buried Alive Never Die* by Karol Truman. The point is that if we don't properly release and heal our emotions, eventually they will manifest in our lives in one form or another. Often it is in the form of an illness or disease - physical, mental, emotional or spiritual. We can come back to a place of peace, healing, forgiveness, joy and even gratitude for our experiences once we know how to properly release and replace these negative emotions.

Whether we like it or not, we are going to go through difficult trials that will not be easy to handle. We will feel that gamut of emotions, and unless you know how to let them go or release them in a healthy way, you will probably stuff them and let them fester and smolder until they become unbearable. You actually may forget about them for years and even decades. But when something comes up in your life and triggers you, you know that there is something going on inside that needs healing. Your life will become unbearable, and you will know that it's time to change.

Teton Dam Flood

Let me give you an analogy that may shine some light on what I'm getting at. When I was 10 years old, I remember a Saturday morning cleaning the house with my mom. You see, I was the ninth of ten children, and my mom ran a tight ship! She had to in order to manage our family. Every Saturday morning we would get up at the crack of dawn to scrub down and clean the house. It was quite the job, but she was creative and would always make some sort of a game of it. Well, this particular Saturday morning I heard a voice coming from a loud speaker of an individual in a Volkswagen Bug driving up and down our street. The words he was saying were, "Get to high ground, the Teton Dam has broken. Get to high ground!"

Even as a young 10-year-old girl, I remember the fright and the concern I felt as I considered the thought that we were going to be flooded. I felt scared. I remember going downstairs to our basement, saying a prayer, and asking for us to be safe. I asked my mom if we could leave, and she wasn't so sure it was a big deal. She thought it might just be some water filling the gutters, so she wanted to be sure we got all of the vacuuming done before we left. I was growing impatient, but we did finish the vacuuming. You've just got to love my mom!

Well, we did make it to high ground, and a few hours later I remember standing at the top of a hill when we saw the wall of water making its way through our small community. It didn't look like water at all. It was brown and muddy. We lived in South Eastern Idaho, and there was farmland all around us. So as the floodwaters made their way down to Rexburg, they picked up everything in its path - cars, homes off their foundations, lumber, cattle, etc. It was quite a sight. I remember standing there watching a home float down the street. Our concern was whether or not our home would still be intact and on its foundation.

Within a few days the water subsided, and we were able to drive to our home. That was a sight and smell I won't ever forget. There was mud and debris everywhere. In our front yard was an overturned car. We lived across the street from a golf course, and there were at least a dozen homes that had landed on the golf course. Mud had filled our basement and come up into our main floor as well. The clean up task ahead was pretty daunting. There was much work that needed to be done to restore our home and our community. Luckily, there were hundreds of busloads of people pouring in to begin helping us with the clean-up. There was a lot of work to get rid of the mess before we could even consider beginning to rebuild our home and community.

After several months, you wouldn't have even have known we experienced a flood. It was cleaned up and had become an even more beautiful community than before. Everyone would agree that even though this experience was so difficult, in the long run our community was transformed into something even better.

Cleaning up our Personal Lives

We experience something similar in our own personal lives. Each of us goes through personal storms or perhaps even floods. Our lives may appear completely devastated or certainly in a big mess that may seem too overwhelming to put back together. But, before we can rebuild our lives, there is an important step that needs to take place. That is clean-up and healing. If we had tried to rebuild our home on top of all of the mud and debris, it wouldn't have worked. It would have become a bigger mess. When we don't take the time in our lives to clean up and clear out the negative emotions and experiences we go through, but simply try to rebuild our lives on top of the pain and heartache, we are setting ourselves up for failure. And we wonder why we are continually stuck!

When people have negative emotions and experiences in their lives, they usually deal with them in one of three ways, none healthy. Often they stuff their feelings and hope that by not dealing with them or paying attention to them, they can eventually make them go away. What actually happens is when we suppress our feelings, they are still alive and begin to fester and cause all sorts of problems that we most likely have no idea are related to the unresolved issues. Suppressed feelings can easily cause anxiety, depression, tension and a host of stress-related problems.

The second way is to express the feeling or emotion. Often a person will lose their temper or blow up. This will relieve the pressure that has accumulated from the negative emotion, and it may even feel good to let it go, but it doesn't get rid of the feeling. Also, there are definitely negative consequences to the individual and to relationships.

Another way to deal with the negative emotion is simply avoidance. People can use distraction to not deal with the issue. They may absorb themselves in work, watching television or turn to emotional eating, drinking or other harmful behaviors.

The most effective way to handle a negative emotion is by focusing on it, experiencing the emotion of it, releasing it, letting it go, and then replacing it with a positive emotion. Anytime we clear or release negative emotion, we must be sure to fill ourselves up with positive things, or we are leaving ourselves vulnerable for the negative to slip back in there.

Once we take an inventory of our lives and do the work for healing to take place, we need to release the negative feelings and experiences that will show up in our lives. As I mentioned earlier, we are human and living in a mortal experience. It is inevitable that things will pop up in our lives, but the key is to immediately take the steps to release so we can keep an open, soft and beautiful heart. This will enable us to have deep and rich, meaningful relationships. It allows us to connect deeply with other people. It just makes our lives more sunny and enjoyable.

I work with individuals one-on-one to do emotional release work and really get to the core of the problems. It is liberating and beautiful to help others in this way, but I want to give you some tools that you'll be able to use on your own. It is empowering to have tools that we can use in our own lives to help us live happy, full and productive lives.

Tools

Writing - F.A.D.E.S.

One method is simply to write. Write out your feelings and put them down on paper. Just write and write until those negative emotions are discharged. It is okay and even desirable to experience the charged emotions as you are writing because this allows you to discharge and release it. It doesn't matter what you write, but just the act of writing gets the emotion out of your body and onto paper. I told you that I like to use acronyms, so in my releasing, I think of the word FADES. That stands for F- frustration, A- anger, D- disappointment, E- embarrassment and S- sadness. I ask myself in the morning if I'm feeling any of those emotions, and if I am, I typically will do some writing to release them.

Once you've written until you no longer feel the negative charge of the emotion, then simply crumple up the paper and throw it away or even burn it. As you do this step, say to yourself, "I release all of these negative emotions, and I replace them with love, forgiveness, joy and peace." Often I will say a prayer to accompany the release. It is important to replace with the positive, otherwise you've just opened up a space within you that may leave you vulnerable to having other negative experiences come in, versus consciously choosing to fill it with the positive.

Emotional Freedom Technique

Another tool to use is Emotion Freedom Technique, commonly called EFT. EFT borrows from the Chinese meridian system. While acupressure and acupuncture have been primarily focused on physical ailments, EFT focuses on emotional issues, which in turn aid the physical issues. EFT combines the physical benefits of acupuncture with the cognitive benefits of talk therapy for a much faster and more complete treatment of emotional issues.

Although related to acupuncture, EFT does not use needles. Instead it is done by focusing in on specific issues and using the fingertips to tap certain meridian points on the body. EFT appears to balance blocks in the meridian system and can be effective in a relatively short amount of time, even minutes. The nice thing about EFT is that it can be done anywhere at any time and can provide impressive do-it-yourself results. You can look EFT up on YouTube and receive step-by-step instruction on how to use it.

Working with Children

I like to use EFT for my young daughters ages 5 and 7, if they have an emotional meltdown or get upset. Often times I'll do some tapping on them while having them repeat my words of release and replace (for example, "I release all of my anger, frustration, sadness or worry and replace it with peace, happiness and joy.") Usually this process results in a giggle fest and within a matter of a couple of minutes, the emotional upset is gone.

Another technique I use on my children to help release negative emotions is to draw a large heart on a piece of paper and talk to them about how their heart is feeling. I have them color out their emotions in the heart. They can scribble and just let out any negative emotions while they are coloring and I'm talking them through it. Once again, I always end by drawing another heart and letting them decorate it to show how much better they are feeling. The two hearts look very different. The latter one is usually decorated and colored in lighter and prettier colors and they'll often put scallops on the happy heart or draw flowers. They can tell that after this little mini process, they do feel better.

Letting Go and Accepting What Is

If you have any young daughters or granddaughters, you have probably watched or listened to the music of the popular movie *Frozen* a few hundred times! This movie had such an impact on children and adults alike. The signature song of the movie is *Let It Go*. This is what we must do to put down the extra emotional baggage that we are carrying around. We may not even realize the emotional baggage we have stuffed in our lives that may be affecting our happiness and energy vibration. I had a really interesting experience that taught me this lesson.

Forgiveness

When I began really learning and implementing these strategies in my life, I had a desire to release as much as I could and began taking an inventory of my life. I started working on all of the emotional issues I could think of and going through my life with a fine-toothed comb. Then I began praying to know if there were things I was missing that I needed to address or forgive.

After I asked specifically to be shown who I needed to forgive in my life to help me find more peace, I had a remarkable experience. For two nights in a row, I had dreams that included my sister's ex-husband and his new wife. After the first night, I thought-wow, that was interesting. I hadn't thought about him for probably ten years! He had left my sister and their five children to marry his secretary. It was a painful time in their lives, and I remember definitely not being happy or liking him or his new wife very much. But that was years earlier, and my sister had gone on and rebuilt her life. I was quite shocked that these two would show up in a dream.

I honestly thought this was my sister's issue and not mine, but I certainly did admit that I was not happy with him or his new wife for the pain that their choices caused my sister and her children. I thought that perhaps I do need to forgive them in my heart. Well, the next night it became very clear as both he and his new wife were in my dream again. I then went through my own process of forgiving them and releasing their choices. I didn't even realize that I had been holding onto a grudge because it had been many years. But obviously my Higher Power knew that I needed to release and forgive. When we hold on to any resentment, we are only hurting ourselves. It keeps us in a negative state and vibration, and we tend to attract more of that into our lives. Just to be able to accept "what is" is very liberating and allows us to let go and live in the present.

Law of Attraction

We don't necessarily attract what we want in our lives, but we attract what we are. For example, if you are constantly and continually giving out love, then you are going to be receiving love. If you are putting out negative vibes towards others then you'll also get that back into your life. So, it seems obvious that we want to put out as much positive into the world as we can. Another favorite book of mine is *Power vs. Force* by David Hawkins, Ph.D. In his book, he has calibrated the energetic level of a variety of emotions. The scale is from 0-1000, with zero being the lowest and 1000 reaching enlightenment. Negative emotions generally range between 0-200. Fear, frustration, shame, sadness, despair, etc. are very low vibrating emotions but as you walk up the scale you find peace, joy, forgiveness, gratitude, love and enlightenment. According to David Hawkins, love calibrates at 600 and enlightenment is 1000. So, related to the law of attraction, we obviously want to fill our hearts and lives with these positive emotions because that is what we are going to attract back to our lives.

Sending Out Love

If you want to influence others, send them your loving energy! In the field of energy, love is one of the highest vibrations. If we master it, we've got happiness by the tail and the power to transform our inner world as well as outer world. That is one of the things that I regularly pray for - pure love. There is evidence that when we raise our own level of love, we radiate that to positively affect our families, communities and ultimately the planet. Sometimes when I see random people out in a grocery store or on a street, I'll send them my love, without words. As we give out love, we receive more of it back into our lives. It is the law of reciprocity. It is our natural state to be loving and vibrant. That is our essence; it is who we are. But often we go into our familiar state, which is more commonplace and habitual - dealing with our own pain and struggle.

I encourage you to try an experiment today. Go throughout your day and think, say and do as many loving things as you can. Then check in to see how you feel and where your emotions are. It is a sure way to raise your energy vibration, lift those around you and just give you an overall warm and cozy feeling inside. When love flows in our lives, it opens up our hearts. It is as if the warm sun is shining down on us and everyone else. We begin to blossom like a flower in the sun. When we withhold our love, our hearts begin to shrivel and close. It is a form of protection from the harshness of life. It is easy to slip into that pattern. That is why on a regular basis I do my own emotional clearing to help open up my heart. Because I've lived both ways, I definitely know that being in the flow of love is where I want to be. Enjoy the warmth and abundance of love today. It starts with you! Start the experiment and witness the happiness of those you touch and watch the love flow right back to you.

Supportive Activity to Nourish Your Heart:

Do daily as needed. Write out on a paper any negative emotions you are feeling. Keep writing until you no longer are feeling the negative emotion. You may want to remember the word F.A.D.E.S. (Frustration, Anger, Disappointment, Embarrassment, Sadness). For example, you would begin writing, "I'm frustrated about……." Go through a variety of negative emotions and write as you feel triggered by any of them. After you've written out your negative emotions, crumple up the paper and throw it away or burn it. I like to imagine in my mind my Higher Power taking those emotions from me. The point is to get those emotions outside your body because *Feelings Buried Alive Never Die*!

Chapter 6

Roots: Nourishing Your Mind

I love this topic! I know the power it can have to transform your life for the better. It can also be used to destroy your life if you are using it incorrectly. If you don't like where your life is right now, all you have to do is take a look at where your thoughts are and what you've been thinking about. We literally are designing our life everyday by our thoughts, so pay close attention and start noticing where your mind is. I'm going to be sharing some powerful tools. If you begin implementing them, I know they can redirect and change your life to whatever you desire it to be. I will be sharing some of my own personal examples and story, but don't just take my word for it. Put this into practice and watch your life transform for the better!

Do you know that we have around 60,000 thoughts daily? Our mind can be our best friend or our worst enemy, and it is within our power to decide which one it will be. One of the great challenges of this life is to be able to control the mind because it can really have a life of its own if we let it go uncontrolled. It takes personal control and discipline to be able to master our thoughts, but believe me, it is worth learning the tools and skills to do this. If you are feeling stuck or discouraged, this one principle will transform your life, if you can master it. What we are really talking about here is creation. We are creators, and we are using our minds to create our lives.

I learned the power of this principle the hard way, but I learned the lesson so well that I'm committed to teach it to others! For the first forty years of my life, it felt like everything in my life flowed to me almost effortlessly. Of course we have everyday challenges, but the majority of my life was easy, effortless, abundant and happy. I don't want to sound arrogant, but almost anything I tried or wanted to have happen in my life did manifest.

I believe that it started because I had a father who totally believed in me and told me that very often. As a young teenage girl, I would have regular father-daughter interviews with him. We would talk about how my life was going, and I would share any concerns that I had. We would set goals together for the things I wanted to accomplish in the next six months. Then at the end of the six months, we would meet again and discuss how those goals went. Something remarkable happened. It seemed like most often, all of my goals were accomplished. I didn't realize it at the time, but he was teaching me a very important principle - accountability. I would come back to him and report how I had done in the specific areas that we discussed. I knew that he knew my desires and goals, and I wanted to meet them and make him proud.

I was very blessed to have a father who totally believed in me and told me that I could do and accomplish anything I wanted. One of the big lessons he ingrained in me as a teenager, who was trying to fit in, was that there were lots of pretty girls out there. But if I wanted to stand out, I should try to be more beautiful on the inside than on the outside. I'll always remember that and how I wanted to make him proud by being beautiful on my inside. Of course, I was concerned how I looked physically as well, but I desired to cultivate a beautiful heart.

So whether it was trying out for cheerleader, winning local pageants, getting good grades, finding jobs, dating, earning scholarships, etc., it seemed like almost anything I wanted would come into my life. It carried over into my married life, and I found the man of my dreams, had wonderful and amazing children, started and ran successful businesses, held leadership positions, etc. I often wondered why people struggled and thought life was so hard. I didn't think or realize I was being judgmental but didn't understand why others seemed to struggle so much.

In this laboratory called life, I had unconsciously learned how to attract everything I desired into my life. I simply believed in myself and that it was possible. Of course it takes work and effort, but my mindset was right. Life really mirrors back to us what our beliefs are. As I mentioned, I had parents who ingrained in me that I could accomplish anything I wanted, so I believed them.

I suppose that I needed to learn many more lessons in life, including a level of compassion for others who struggled with difficult challenges. Everything shifted for me when I was forty years old and lost my daughter. You see, I was really born to be a mother. I desperately wanted children throughout my life. Even though there were ten children in the family I grew up in, I was number nine and always wanted more younger siblings to play with. I used to beg my mom to have another baby so I could take care of the baby. Of course, she told me that would not be happening. So, I was thrilled to be able to start my own family and become a mother.

I remember consciously deciding to be the best mother I possibly could. I took this role very seriously, and I absolutely loved being a mom. Of course motherhood came with challenges, but I really gave it all of my energy. I even began homeschooling my children because I began imagining all of the wonderful things we could do as a family. We would have morning devotionals, memorize scriptures, read classics and study inspiring heroes. We took field trips and had hands-on learning. Instead of simply studying about the founding of America, we traveled and did an American history tour and visited Mount Vernon, Gettysburg, walked the Boston trail and saw and experienced so many other sights. We studied great heroes, had book clubs, took art classes and really created a wonderful community with other families to experience the joy of learning, building our character and strengthening family.

So when my sweet and beloved daughter passed away in her sleep following a brief illness, I was unprepared for the heartache, trauma, pain and devastation. She was a treasured gift to our family, and it was through a deeply spiritual process that she was brought into our home. Not only was my heart broken into a million pieces, but my sense of worth as a person and her mother who had the charge of caring for her was destroyed.

I was immediately blessed following her passing with some beautiful, spiritual witnesses and gifts. I was given a great amount of light and comfort. I thank the Lord for these tender mercies because I don't know if I could have survived without them. I barely survived, as it was. I would hold onto the knowledge I was being given, the love that poured into our family and the light that was teaching me through this experience, but then my mind started going in all sorts of directions. I had never struggled with my thoughts before, but now it felt like a thousand negative thoughts were streaming into my head at once. "I must be a terrible mother... If only I would have done this... What if I would have done that... I must be a disappointment to God and my family..." and on and on.

I had never experienced such discouragement, which later spiraled into a clinical depression a couple years after her passing. I was desperately trying to hold onto the light but I felt as if I was also being pulled down into a black hole, and I didn't know how to get out. I don't want to spend much time describing the darkness and depression, but I will simply say that I was in for a whole new journey and learning experience. I needed to try to get my life back, but I had no idea how. I was lucky to have some heroes and angels in my life who stepped in to get me some medical help and intervention. This was a blessing in my life, but there would be a long road of recovery ahead of me. Fighting with my thoughts was a continual battle, and I felt like there was a war within me between light and hope and darkness and despair.

Suddenly my level of compassion for those who had gone through difficult, challenging or traumatic events in their lives skyrocketed a thousand percent. No wonder other people struggled. How do you deal with your life when you have devastating experiences happen? I wasn't sure, but I knew that I needed to figure it out. I needed to get my life back. And when something changes me, I can't keep my mouth shut about it. I desperately want to share it with others to help their lives improve as well. I needed to find tools to use on a daily basis to help me with my thinking.

Power of Creation

One morning as I was up early and contemplating how to move forward, I had a very empowering thought and idea come to my mind. I knew that I had created the hell that I had been living in through all of the things I had been telling myself and then began to believe about myself. I knew it was these thoughts that had taken me down to a very dark place. Well, that meant if I could create a hell in my own life, then I had the power to create the most wonderful life I could imagine through my thoughts as well. The idea of this became very exciting to me. It would put me back in control of my life and not allow my thoughts to play havoc with my mind or my life. I admit that it is easier said than done, and it has been quite the journey coming back, but it is possible, and I've found some treasured nuggets of knowledge and tools along the way.

When I was in the pit and in my darkest hour, I didn't believe anything positive about myself. So, I decided if I was to recreate my life, then I would need to borrow from the admirable traits of other women that I looked up to. I began thinking of women that had made an impact in my life and the traits that I admired about them. I started listing two traits for each person. These became my affirmations. Once I wrote them down, I began memorizing them so I could recall them at a moment's notice.

Now I had a tool to use when my thoughts would begin taking me to a bad place. I could just rattle off my affirmations. I began saying them first thing in the morning when I woke up and also saying them before I went to bed at night. Sometimes I would say them while I was driving or just whenever I needed to refocus my mind. Many people have asked me for my affirmations. They are personal to me and have evolved over time, but I will tell you what they are to give you an idea. Once again, at the time I wrote them, I didn't believe these things about myself, but I knew that I needed to rewire my brain with new and good thoughts and beliefs. I knew that by repeatedly saying them and focusing on them, I could ingrain them into my subconscious brain which would then help me become that person again.

Affirmations

These are my affirmations: "I am Stacy Larsen Harmer; I am pure and virtuous; I am an incredible wife and mother; I am self motivated and self disciplined; I am a devoted daughter of God and a faithful follower of Jesus Christ; I am loving and vibrant; I am giving and compassionate; I am sweet and gentle; I am strong and determined; I am helpful and healing; I am fit and lean; I am smart and articulate; I am clean and organized; I am inspiring and influential; I am beautiful and talented." I have many more, but I'll stop there. These words are ingrained in me, as I've said them almost daily for the past seven years. I created them using my conscious brain, which is about 5% of our brain capacity. But, by saying them daily and focusing on them repeatedly, they've gone into my subconscious brain, which is really the powerhouse of our brains and about 95% of our brain capacity. That is when our beliefs change. Whatever is in our subconscious brain really rules our lives. That is why habits are so much stronger than desire. Habits are ingrained into our subconscious brain.

I've witnessed in myself how powerful words are for good or for bad and how we can create the life we want by the beliefs that we have and the words we speak. I was born with this knowledge in me and was fortunate to have parents who truly believed I could accomplish anything and ingrained it in me. But I had to relearn it after my life fell apart. Through experimenting on this with my own life, I can see how people get stuck and struggle. Often they don't know how to get out of their own pit. They focus on the negative things going on in their lives and try to "figure it out." But, as long as we do this, we are giving energy, thought, worry and words to all the bad that is going on, which in turn, will only bring more bad into our lives.

Power of Intention

One of the most effective ways to use our thoughts is to create our positive intentions. We do this by stating our goals, ideas, wants, desires and choices in the affirmative. Louise Hay's book, *I Can Do It*, is a great resource to give you lots of ideas of positive affirmations in many areas of your life. Once we set our intentions on doing a specific thing, something magical happens. It's as if the universe joins us in partnership and will bring those opportunities to us. If you've never experimented with this principle, I'd encourage you to get detailed about a specific intention. Write it down; visualize it; focus on it; imagine it happening. Then get busy doing what needs to be done. Something powerful begins pulling all the energy in the universe to bring about your specific desire. I'd like to give you a couple of examples of how this has worked in my life.

Law of Attraction

As I was striving to rebuild my life after dealing with my depression, I was introduced to a woman named Carol Tuttle. A dear friend of mine brought me her book, *Remembering Wholeness*. I was hungry for anything that could help me on my path forward, and her words were very powerful for me. I began wanting to learn more from her, so I think I purchased all that she had to offer in the form of courses and CD's.

She was creating a program, *Dressing Your Truth*, and I went through her workshop. I loved everything I learned from her, and I decided that somehow I wanted to be associated with her. I didn't know what that looked like, but I knew that I wanted to be associated with her some way. So, I put her *Dressing Your Truth* brochure up on my dream board, a board with visual images or words that you focus on daily to help bring those particular things to pass in your life.

I would look at my dream board every morning and evening and imagine those things actually happening. I would feel the emotion and excitement of it occurring in my life. Well, before long, I was contacted by Carol and asked to be a guest on her Radio Show. This was fun for me, and I was able to share my story with her audience. Then before long, I was contacted and asked if I would participate and allow my picture to be used in her *Dressing Your Truth* materials. I went for a photo shoot, and then was interviewed. My photos and video are used on her promotional materials. After all of this happened, I thought, "Wow! That came about because I had a clear intention." I didn't know what would happen. We don't need to know all the details; we just need to be clear on our desires.

Another fun example happened when I was at a convention. There were around 10,000 people at this event, and I heard a speaker share his experience about climbing Mount Everest. He was putting together an expedition to climb Kilimanjaro. During the time of my darkest hour, my husband gave up a trip that he had planned to Kilimanjaro to stay by my side and help me recover. I thought that I would love to be able to help him find a way to do that trip again. I really wanted to speak with this man, and tried to find him after his speech but couldn't. I decided that I would put all of this new intention and law of attraction stuff I had been learning to the test. I specifically remember stating that I wanted to bring him to me, so I could talk with him. There were thousands of people and many break-out sessions.

I didn't see him that day. But when I came back the next day for the convention, I went to one of many breakout sessions that were being held. It was a large room that probably held 1000 seats. I took a seat by myself and there were empty seats around me, but people were filling in. As I was deep in thought, who should come sit down in the very seat right next to me? It was this very gentleman that I had desired to discuss

Kilimanjaro with. Of all of the different sessions he could attend, and all of the thousands of seats he could have chosen, he sat in the seat right next to me. I didn't need to frantically find him; he came to me after I had made the intention that I needed to connect with him. I was able to discuss his climbing expedition and get contact information for a possible future climb for my husband.

Feng Shui Principles

Let me share one last example on the power of our intentions. For several months, I had studied Feng Shui principles to enrich my home life. This is an ancient art of decorating and placement based on the idea that everything in your outer surroundings affects you. One applies it in their inner life through techniques like meditation, positive thinking and creating balance and harmony in your mind, body and spirit. It also uses the Bagua, a Feng Shui map, to locate the energy centers in your home to enhance everything from your relationships to your career.

Well, I decided to do an experiment. My husband, Matt, was orchestrating and working on a very complex transactional deal with his company and had been working hard for several months. We rarely saw him home before 10:00 pm, and he had spent the previous week negotiating in New York. He found himself in the middle of the economic crisis several years ago and the deal began turning sour. I decided to put what I had been studying to the test! According to Feng Shui, each area of your home represents an area of your life. When there is clutter and disorder in a particular area, the corresponding life area will also be stuck or simply not thriving. I stopped and took a look at the Prosperity and Abundance center in our home. It happened to be our back entry from the garage and laundry room. I was a bit chagrined to recognize the disarray. I had loads of unfinished laundry, piles of shoes, coats, backpacks, stacks of unwanted papers, etc. I thought to myself; I'm going to completely transfigure this area of my home (Prosperity and Abundance) to see if I might aid in getting Matt's transaction accomplished.

I spent two full days catching up and clearing out the area. I didn't stop there. I redecorated it using color, water, fragrance, plants, etc. Well, the very next day Matt came home after a long conference call involving attorneys across the country, and the deal was done!! Hallelujah! I told him afterwards what I had been doing, and my cute husband stated that to whatever effect it may have had...."*Thank You*". I'm not claiming any credit, but I do know when there is a clear intent, the energy flow moves, and with God's grace, miracles can happen.

There is one caveat to all of this. We have to believe it will happen! If deep down inside us we say, this would never work, then it probably won't. It's like it cancels out the order. The law of attraction is really the law of the harvest. We reap what we sow. Before the law of gravity was identified, everyone was still affected by it. It is the same with the law of attraction. Whatever we put our attention on will come back to us multiplied. That is why so many people find themselves stuck or in a funk. They focus on their problems and what is not working in their life. Be careful with the words you use because whatever you say to yourself or others becomes your reality.

Dream Boards

Creating a dream or vision board is a fun and powerful way to create the life you desire. It is a visual representation of what you want your life to be. I've been using Dream Boards for the past seven years and have had wonderful results. You take pictures and words that represent your desires and place them on a board. Then you look and focus on it morning and night for a few minutes at a time. As you do, imagine in your mind these things actually coming to pass. Feel the anticipation and excitement when they do. When we tie our emotion into our thoughts, our intentions become even more powerful. Also, simply repeatedly focusing on the images imprints them into our subconscious, which is the powerhouse of our brains. It becomes a combination of the power of the subconscious, the law of attraction and simple reminders for the action steps we need to take to bring about the results we desire.

I had a wonderful experience with my Dream Board recently. At the end of December, I created my Dream Board for the new year. On it, I included many things in several areas of my life. I had posted a picture stating that I wanted to speak at a specific Retreat for women, sharing these tools I'm including in this book. I hadn't mentioned it to anyone, but within a few weeks, the organizer called asking me to speak. They flew me to Arizona, put me up in a wonderful hotel, and I had a life-changing experience, as I was able to speak to 500 dynamic women entrepreneurs.

Your board should include all areas of your life that you want to improve. It may include health and fitness, relationships, spirituality, personal development, travel, career, goals, dreams, etc. Have fun dreaming, discovering, cutting, and creating your Dream Board and manifesting your desires!!

Movie Script

Another fun tool is to write a movie script for your life five years down the road. You write out a very detailed day of what your ideal life looks like. Be specific about where you are, who you are with, what you are doing and the impact you are having.

When a mentor gave me this challenge, I followed his encouragement and wrote out my movie script. Something amazing happened as I was creating my ideal life and writing it out. I had just written down that I would be holding retreats for women and speaking and sharing my principles of Vibrant Living. As I was literally writing this, I received a telephone call from a friend. She was creating an organization and would be holding retreats for women. She asked if I would be on her board and if I would come speak at her retreat. I have not had something manifest that quickly before, and it was a very cool reminder about the power of our intentions and desires. When we get the negative thinking and emotions out of the way, anything is possible!!

Essential Tools to Keep Your Mind in Tip Top Shape

I've shared many ideas and principles to nourish your mind. The whole idea is to reprogram your brain, create new neural pathways, get positive thoughts and habits into your subconscious and be clear with your intentions. With all of these great principles, you are sure to have a powerful reservoir of tools to use regularly in creating the life you want. Yet, there are some essential points to remember when you are implementing these ideas. Believe me, I've practiced all of them. My own life has been a laboratory for everything I'm sharing with you. If you implement the principles I've shared with you in this chapter, you are sure to get some good results. But in order to get great results, you need to make sure your mind is free and clear.

Let me illustrate what I mean. Have you ever used a calculator? You do a series of calculations into one problem and come up with an answer. But, then to move on to the next problem, you must clear the calculator to get the correct answer. If you just run problems into problems into problems, you'll have a whole jumbled mess of numbers that won't make any sense. It is very similar with our minds. It is important that we clear our calculator, or mind, continually. Otherwise, we are mixing and compounding our old problems with new problems.

Stillness

One way we can do this is to be completely still. In the next chapter, I'm going to go much more in depth on meditation, but this practice has literally changed my life in amazing ways. I'm excited to share with you how in the next chapter. But, for now, to help clear our minds, we need to be able to control our thoughts. There were so many times when I felt as if my thoughts were spinning out of control. It was exhausting, and I'd get so frustrated with myself. I had to learn to hold a thought for a period of time to calm my mind.

Once I adopted this practice, my peace increased a hundred fold. I thought of a sweet experience in my life that brought me great joy, and when I found my thoughts slipping and getting out of control, I would concentrate on this moment. Since so many of my negative thoughts were related to losing my daughter, I would focus on the moment she was placed into my arms as we were standing in the Seattle airport. She had been escorted from Korea with a sweet woman, and I remember this little bundle of joy with a full head of black hair. I've given birth to 5 children, and having Olivia placed in my arms at that moment was no different in bonding than giving birth and having my babies placed in my arms. It was an exquisite moment of joy after the long and hard labor of adoption, and anyone who has ever gone through that knows what I mean! In fact, I remember someone saying to me once how easy that must have been not going through a pregnancy and labor. But, I responded that it was harder than all of my pregnancies and labors put together, albeit I had easy pregnancies and labors.

So, I would encourage you to remember a time in your life that brought you great joy. Just try to hold on to that thought for a period of time, especially if your mind starts taking you to a negative place. You need to stop it in its tracks. This is really the first step of meditation, that ability to slow down your mind, breathe deeply and come to a place of peace.

Accepting What Is

Another essential tool for clearing your mind is to accept the past and what is. Once you do this, you will become empowered to move forward and create whatever life you desire. When we hold onto regret, guilt, sadness, anger or despair, it is impossible to move forward and rebuild our lives. We all make mistakes, and we must be loving and forgiving of ourselves. There is no point in worrying about the past or mistakes we may have made. I know it is easier said than done. Believe me, I've played over in my mind a thousand times, "If only I had done this," or, "If only I had done that".

I want to tell you right now from my own experience, it does you no good! There is nothing good or positive in the wishing that something were different. It also keeps us from living and enjoying the present moment. That is where we must be in order to live a full and happy life. If we are worrying about the past or even worrying about the future, which we have no control over, it is a whole lot of worry and it just messes with our brains and happiness. By simply accepting what is and finding your happy place, you'll have much more peace and contentment. Once again, if you find your thoughts slipping out of control, which can quickly bring you down, take a deep breath, be still and remember that moment of great joy in your life and hold on to it.

Remove Negativity

Have you ever met someone who simply loves to live in the negative? It can be very draining and can certainly bring down your spirits. Negativity is like a poison, and it begins to darken everything it touches. If a child constantly hears from a parent about all the things they are doing wrong, how does that ever change the child? It simply lowers their self-esteem and self worth, and soon the child may believe that they must not be good enough. I've worked with many people, and it seems like one of the core issues so many people are dealing with is that they feel they are not enough. It usually goes back to when they were children and felt as if they couldn't or didn't measure up. It really taints every other aspect of their lives if they have this as a core belief.

That is why it is so important to reprogram negative thoughts and beliefs into the truth. The truth is that our eternal nature, or essence, is perfect. We may make mistakes, but that is what this earth life is for. We are here to learn the lessons that we must learn, and most of us learn those from experience - good or bad. Sometimes it takes hitting rock bottom to realize that this is NOT where we want to end up. My wonderful sister always says that if you find yourself at rock bottom, you have a pretty strong foundation to build your life back up.

It is essential to our happiness that we remove any negative thoughts about others or ourselves. It does us no good at all. In fact, it is harmful. David Shaw, in his groundbreaking book, *The Bug Free Mind*, states that the more negativity one has, the bigger the ego. Our goal is to remove our ego and surrender. That is when and where you'll find your true peace and power from within.

Supportive Activity to Nourish Your Mind:

In the left column, write out any negative statements that pop into your mind about yourself. In the right column, counteract them by making your **POWER DECLARATIONS**. These are the exact opposite statements written in present tense. For example, "I am not good enough," and directly across from that statement, write the **TRUTH IN PRESENT TENSE** – "I am strong, capable, and am deserving of all good things in my life."

Negative Self Talk	**POWER DECLARATIONS**

Chapter 7

Roots: Nourishing Your Spirit

My daughter Olivia loved butterflies. In fact, after her passing, we were given a sweet picture covered with butterflies and flowers that she had drawn in her preschool. At the end of her graveside service, we had all of the people let go of butterflies and there were dozens and dozens of beautiful butterflies fluttering up to the sky. A butterfly is a lovely creature that emerges from the dark isolated cocoon. It symbolizes transformation. I believe we are spiritual beings having a mortal experience on this earth, and hopefully through the experiences of mortality we transform our lives into something beautiful. It may take a while, but we have a lifetime.

From my experience, nourishing your Spirit is the best way to aid in that personal transformation. When we can let go of our ego and strive to live in our true Essence, we begin to discover who we are and who we have always been. It may be rocky at times, and we will each go through trials that may test us beyond what we think we are capable of experiencing. Through this journey of mortality, hopefully we will learn the lessons we are meant to learn. In the end, I believe it will be about the lessons and understanding we have gained, and how fully we have learned to love.

I admire C.S. Lewis' insights and writings. He struggled to understand how an omnipotent Being could allow such suffering in the world. Lewis suffered much pain in his life. But, with the change of his worldview from atheism to Christianity, he looked at God as a good, conscientious surgeon: "The kinder and more conscientious he is, the more inexorably he will go on cutting. If he yielded to your entreaties, if he stopped before the operation was complete, all the pain up to that point would have been useless."

Even amidst trials and tribulations, there is peace to be found. It is finding the light within each one of us. There are many sources that would like to dim that light, but we were not meant for failure.

A great spiritual teacher once asked, "What is the greatest need in the world?" The wise student responded, "Is not the greatest need in all of the world for every person to have a personal, ongoing, daily continuing relationship with Deity?" Having such a relationship can unchain the divinity within us, and nothing can make a greater difference in our lives as we come to know and understand our divine relationship with God or our Higher Power.

I had always strived to be a good person and did believe in Jesus Christ, but I realized that in many ways I had been asleep for the first forty years of my life. I suppose I could describe the period in my life after losing Olivia as sort of a spiritual awakening. My spiritual journey is deeply personal, but I'm going to share bits and pieces of it to help illustrate the points I'm trying to make.

The morning that we lost her, we were all in such a state of shock and disbelief. We were devastated, and the lives that we knew were never to be the same. Our hearts were crushed into a million pieces, but we were also unprepared for the outpouring of love that started flowing into our lives, both from our dear family and friends as well as blessings from the Lord. My sweet husband had called my sister immediately to come to my side. He was so concerned about me and wanted to have her by my side during this trying time. He knew that she would know how to comfort me since she, too, had lost her own daughter several years earlier.

After they took Olivia from our home, my husband gathered our family upstairs in our bedroom to say a family prayer. I can't remember the words that he spoke, but during the prayer, I was granted an incredibly sweet and tender experience. Prior to this time in my life, I was unaware of any spiritual gifts I might have, but during this prayer a vision unfolded before my eyes - even though they were closed. I saw my sweet little Olivia in the arms of her cousin, Lexi, my oldest sister's daughter. They were embracing and spinning round and round together as if they were weightless. It looked like they were laughing and giggling. They definitely looked happy. Then the spinning stopped, and my Olivia looked at me and gave me a thumbs up.

I sat there quite stunned at the experience. I had never had anything remotely similar happen to me in my life, and I know there are many people that have lost loved ones that long for those experiences. It was a sweet blessing and privilege that I was so grateful for because I didn't know if I could survive the devastation of losing her. I immediately ran downstairs to tell my sister Collette, and her daughter, Sharlie about the experience of seeing Olivia and Lexi together.

For some time I pondered on that sacred experience. I was so grateful but also hungry for more. If the Lord was willing to grant me that, what else would He grant me? I hung on to hope from that tender mercy because before long I would be a puddle of tears and so very devastated. I went from great amounts of light and understanding to pain, darkness and despair.

Later that morning, I remember going and finding a quiet place to be alone and pray. I poured out my soul to my Father in Heaven, and then a thought came to my mind. The thought was of Jesus Christ, and my belief that He had atoned for every mortal on earth. Then the thought came to me to petition Him to allow the Atonement to heal our lives and make something positive from this very heartbreaking situation. I pled that His Atonement could make it better. As I uttered these words, a warm and beautiful feeling embraced my whole body from head to toe, and I felt like everything was gong to be okay. I didn't know how, but I knew that He was in charge.

In the days and weeks following, I began looking for signs of His and Olivia's love. I found it in every beautiful flower I saw, every bird or butterfly that fluttered by. I saw it in the beautiful sunrises and sunsets, and even though my heart was broken, it was also expanding as I began seeing God's hand in all the beauty of the earth around us. I began filling my heart with gratitude for every gift and little remembrance of my daughter, and as I did this, I began to see them all around me.

At night I couldn't sleep, so I would wake up around 2 am, and go downstairs to my living room. We had a picture of the Savior hanging on our wall. I needed someone to pour my heart out to, and so I began getting the picture off the wall and putting it down near me on the floor and I would just talk, cry, plead and pour my heart out. I can't explain why this helped me, but I felt the Savior becoming very personal to me.

He was tangible and accessible. I felt deeply of His love and knew that He knew exactly how I felt. He not only died for the sins of everyone, His Atonement covered every heartache, pain, mistake and injustice. I felt an outpouring of love like I never had experienced in my life. I wondered if it took losing my child to gain this type of understanding. I realized very personally that I was nothing without my Savior. I was powerless without Him, but when He was at my side, I could accomplish anything I wanted and all was perfect.

Meditation

Before this time, I had always been very busy. I could accomplish a great deal in a short amount of time. I was a go-getter, very independent and had relied much on my own strength. But, now everything had changed. I felt broken. I had always soared through life almost effortlessly but now my wings were damaged. When a bird's wings are damaged, that bird is put into a dark box, and after time passes, the wing is able to repair itself. Well, my wings were broken and now instead of soaring, I slowed way down and went into a dark box for healing. Life seemed to stop for me. I remember going to Costco just a few days after Olivia's passing and wondering how everyone could be hustling and bustling around so busily. Didn't they know that life had just come to a complete halt and the world had lost a precious angel? Even though the world carried on busily around me, suddenly my life was slowing down dramatically.

It was at this time that I was in great need of comfort, that I began meditating. This is something I had never done before, but I had a great desire to connect with my daughter spiritually. The best way I could think of doing this was to go to a quiet place. I would lie down, empty out all of my thoughts, and breathe deeply. I had a great desire to connect with her and the Lord. I would imagine myself as an empty vessel that was open to receiving all that the Lord would give me. After doing this on a regular basis every morning and evening, beautiful experiences began happening to me. It was as if I was able to transcend this mortal experience and connect spiritually beyond the veil. The Lord started pouring out beautiful blessings to me, and I was hungry for them. I was so grateful for any spiritual connection I would receive and continually desired more. It taught me in a very personal way how important it was to quiet our minds and deeply connect with the Divine. It truly was transforming my life and understanding.

Journaling

In addition to meditating and receiving beautiful spiritual gifts and witnesses, I would write down the experiences I had. I wanted the Lord to know how grateful I was for the experiences and spiritual connections I was having and that I never wanted to forget them. I would record them in a journal. As I began this practice, I learned another principle. It seemed like the more I recorded these experiences, the more often they came. It was as if it was opening up a continual door of revelation. I now have over a dozen filled journals and hundreds of typed pages of my own recordings of spiritual experiences. Each of these principles I'm sharing is extremely important, but I would highly encourage you to begin keeping a record or journal of inspiration and spiritual experiences you have. Experiment, and see if they don't increase. I try to remember to express my gratitude for any bit of knowledge, light or understanding I am given, and it seems to keep the door continually open.

Lucid Dreams

At this time I also began discovering Lucid Dreaming. This is a state that you are in where you are not quite in deep sleep but you aren't fully awake either. It is a place between the unconscious and consciousness. I have found that it is a state where I can be taught great and marvelous things if I go to bed with a desire and question in my mind. In fact, I felt like I needed to cleanse my life so I would continue to have these personal spiritual experiences with my daughter and others. I began taking an inventory of my life. Who did I need to forgive, and whom did I need to seek forgiveness from? When I prayed and asked these questions, I was shown and taught things, such as the dream I had to forgive my former brother-in-law and his new wife.

I'm sharing this simply as an example of how we can be taught things if we desire. There are many different type of spiritual gifts, and dreams is one of them. Of course, I always record the experiences that I have and what I am taught in my journal. And as I mentioned previously, the more

I show gratitude and appreciation for what I am given, the more spiritual experiences I have.

Connect to the Divine Daily

How do you come closer to God and put Him first in your life? I say that you start by putting him first in your days. The early morning hours are so sacred to me. It is during this quite time that I can connect best with my Higher Power. My head is much more clear and the busyness of the day hasn't begun. It is during this time that I pray, meditate, study my scriptures, record in my journal and just have a beautiful communion time. This is part of my daily morning routine. I don't set an alarm, but my body just wakes up, most often very early. It is not uncommon for me to be up at 4 am with a few hours of my own before the day starts in my home.

Other ways I connect with the Divine often include listening to uplifting music, walking in nature and simply having a prayer in my heart throughout the day. I treat Him as my constant companion, and I know that by partnering with Him, I can do all things through Him.

Spiritual Awakening

Life never stands still and neither do our personal lives. Are we moving forward and progressing, or are we backsliding? It is not uncommon to be off course a good amount of time. But, as we seek for a final destination, we can navigate and come back into alignment quickly. A plane is off the exact course probably 90% of the times during a flight, but the pilot knows its final destination and nearly always arrives there. The same is true for our lives. We must have the ability to continually get our lives back on track when we make inevitable mistakes. That is part of the journey. The more mistakes we make, the more opportunities we have for success because at least we are trying.

I am a recovering perfectionist. There was a time in my life where I held myself to an impossible spiritual standard, and it nearly drove me crazy. When we accept that this mortal experience is about learning and progression, we can be kinder to ourselves and appreciate that we learn with every action and mistake we make. Now, instead of focusing on perfection, I focus on progress. Am I making more progress today than yesterday?

As we become spiritually awakened, our very natures change. Some signs of this are the following:

1. You feel love for no reason. It is easy to see the beauty of life all around you. Love is a verb, and you desire to be of service to others. You let go of judgment, and give others the benefit of the doubt. You show kindness and generosity to yourself and others.

2. You focus on the present moment. You've forgiven the past and accept what is. You aren't overly concerned about the future and realize that the present moment is what counts.

3. You are happy. You can look past the negative and strive to be in a positive place. If you do feel negative feelings or get stressed, you have tools to get you out of that space and can turn it around quickly.

4. You desire deep, meaningful relationships and interactions. You won't be satisfied with the superficial but desire to know and understand others at a deeper level.

5. You trust that things are working out for your highest good and will work out perfectly in your life. You don't get overly stressed or anxious about things. If you do, you have tools to help you slow down, back up, breathe and become present.

6. You take accountability. You don't blame others for your circumstances, and you feel capable of creating things for yourself. You feel gratitude for the lessons you've learned.

7. You see that the purpose of life is to learn lessons. You understand and accept that everyone is on his or her own path and will learn the lessons they are meant to learn on this journey.

As you embark on a journey to deepen your connection to the Divine, your life will never be the same. The fruits that come from this area in your life are truly amazing and life changing.

Supportive Activity to Nourish Your Spirit:

Fill your heart with gratitude for what you already have in your life. Answer the questions below. Get into a habit of either recording daily a few things you are grateful for or simply say them during your quiet meditation time.

Gratitude

Three great things I love about my physical body are:

Three people that have had a profound impact on my life are:

Three things I love about where I live are:

Three gifts or talents I've been given are:

Three ways I've been lucky in my life are:

Three ways that my life is abundant and prosperous:

Chapter 8

Trunk: Setting up Systems and Structure

The trunk of the tree symbolizes structure - setting up systems for the various roles that we have. This is step 5 of the seven steps. In the previous chapters we focused on ourselves and nourishing our bodies, hearts, minds and souls on a daily basis. Now, we move on to examine the different roles that we play and responsibilities we have. When there is order and structure in our lives, everything seems to run more smoothly. Setting up systems streamlines our efforts in the many roles we have in our lives. S.Y.S.T.E.M. stands for Save Your Self Time Energy and Money. It really does do that. Although it takes mental energy to initially set them up, it frees up your mind and energy to not have to think about all the details repeatedly.

I really like this step because I need it in my life. I admit that I thrive in structure. I'm not a fly-by-the-seat-of-my-pants type of gal. I like to make plans, set goals, and know where I'm going. I like to think of myself as an organized person, but it isn't something that comes second nature to me or is very easy. Because of this, I've spent a great amount of time and effort putting order and systems in my life. I'm certainly not perfect at it, but it is all about progress, not perfection. If we wait until something is perfectly set up, we will never make any progress and we'll be stuck waiting. That is the trap many people find themselves in, so I suggest you start where you are. Give yourself some credit and simply start moving forward. I've heard it said that anything worth doing is worth doing poorly at first. It is often through our mistakes that we figure out a better way to do things. We don't want to become paralyzed because we are afraid something isn't perfect.

Because I am a wife and mother first and foremost, I've needed some systems to help keep my home running smoothly. I have a fairly large family, so sometimes the schedules, activities, carpooling and responsibilities of keeping on top of everything can be a bit overwhelming. A couple of great resources I've used in helping me create systems and order in my life are *Fly Lady* and *The Power of Moms*. Their web sites offer a plethora of great information and resources to help with setting up systems in your home and for incoming paper management.

It really is quite impossible to organize clutter, so the key is to simplify and clear the excess clutter from our lives, homes and mind. When we have physical clutter around us, the energy in our environments gets stuck, and because everything is a mirror, we feel personally stuck in our lives. When we have an excess of mind clutter, we may feel confused and overwhelmed and have a difficult time making decisions or seeing things very clearly. Have you ever felt paralyzed because you've simply got too much to do? We often get overwhelmed and simply do nothing.

Darren Hardy, a personal development and success guru, gives an example of a lion and a lion tamer. A lion is a ferocious animal, and if you were in a den or a cage with a lion, it would likely attack you. So, how does a lion tamer control a lion into inaction so it becomes docile? He has a four-legged stool pointing at the lion. The lion now has four prongs pointing at him, and he goes from a ferocious beast to completely docile. This illustrates how as individuals we may become paralyzed if we have too many different projects or demands pointing directly at us without any system for management. Paralysis sets in and inhibits our ability to move forward

In order to avoid this, breaking down our lives into bite-size chunks and setting up systems is the key to a calm, peaceful mind and life. Also, by taking on one task or thing at a time, we become more focused and successful and can get many more things accomplished in a quicker amount of time.

When I have order in my life, everything seems to flow beautifully. When there is no order, things fall into chaos pretty quickly. Because I've lived in both chaos and order and prefer my life to flow smoothly, I've come up with ideas and systems (or borrowed ideas from others) that work for me. I will explain and share a few of the systems and ideas that I have found helpful and also share resources where you can go much more in depth.

Schedule Everything on your Calendar

Marie Forleo, a mentor and founder of the popular online Business School says to schedule everything on your calendar. If it is not written down and scheduled, it is not real. I have found it very helpful to use both my iPhone calendar and a paper calendar to keep my schedule. I like my iPhone because it will send me reminder notices on my phone before a scheduled event. Since I am very visual, I also like to be able to see a paper calendar with everything scheduled to help me see the bigger picture.

Do CPR on your home

In Debbie Lillard's book, *A Mom's Guide to Home Organization*, she describes doing CPR on your home. CPR stands for Categorize, Purge and Rearrange. I feel a physical weight around my shoulders when there is too much stuff and clutter in my life. Few things will free me as much as a good de-cluttering. Moving is a good excuse to really go through your things and reorganize, but most of us don't move every year (although I did for the first 11 years of my marriage). When I do a room, closet or box, I will categorize the items, then purge as much as possible, then rearrange them in a more suitable fashion. I have purchased many clear storage containers that fit my shelving spaces, and I've used those containers to help me rearrange stuff and get things more organized. The reorganization is helpful, but the key really is the purging. Every item we have in our home should bring us some type of joy and happiness. If we are holding on to things that have no meaning or purpose and don't necessarily add joy to our lives, appreciate the item for the use you've had of it over the years and allow it to bless someone else's life who could use it more than you. This is an incredibly liberating process. Just sit back and watch: as you create more flow and space in your home, your life will change for the better. If you need additional help on home organization, I would highly recommend *Fly Lady*.

Yearly, Quarterly, Monthly, Weekly and Daily Goals

One of the most powerful tools I've used is simply writing to get ideas and thoughts out of my brain and onto paper. This creates space in brains for more ideas to come as well. Make a list of everything you need or would like to do. Then set five year, one year, quarterly, monthly, and weekly goals. When we lay it out like this, we can see that we can have it all - just not all at the same time! Sometimes I feel like I want to accomplish all of my dreams and desires right now, and then I end up putting way too much on my plate. Once I get things written out and can see a bigger picture, everything becomes more doable. I can enjoy the journey, live in the present moment, and focus on one thing at a time.

It is much more likely that we will accomplish something if it is written down. In fact, only around 3% of the population actually writes down goals. Once a goal is written down, it gets programmed into our subconscious brain, especially if we focus on it. We are then much more likely to accomplish it.

I like to divide my goals into yearly, quarterly, monthly, weekly, and daily goals. As we participate in this activity, we can pace ourselves in a realistic way that works best for our family. We don't need to beat ourselves up for not getting more accomplished but just understand that there is a perfect time to do everything. Five, three and one-year goals help you to see the bigger picture and how to fit your desires and interests into your life. Quarterly goals give you three months to work on a larger project that you've been meaning to do but never find the time. When I know that I have three months to accomplish something larger, then I can pace myself and not get discouraged if I make just incremental steps. I use my quarterly goals for things such as performing CPR on my home (categorize, purge and re-arrange), organizing photos, putting together a scrapbook/photo book, etc.

Monthly goals are just smaller items that need a shorter time frame. I set a monthly goal to revamp my menus and grocery lists. Once, I was so excited about it that I got it done in just a couple of days, but I had given myself the space of a month to accomplish it. You repeat the process for your weekly and daily goals. I'll go more into how I like to structure my weekly and daily schedule later in this chapter.

Every Sunday evening, we hold a family council. In addition to covering specific topics with our children, we calendar the week. I also do my own planning session on Sunday for the upcoming week. I am flexible with my planning, but I have more time to play with my kids and do the important things when I do my planning. Otherwise, I just feel a weight that things aren't getting done that need attention.

Establish an AM/PM Routine

This is simply a checklist of items that I do to begin and end my day. It creates structure and really helps get my days off to a good start. It also brings it around full circle as I end my days. Some of the things I have listed for my AM routine are: meditation (I do this as soon as I wake up in the morning), visualization, affirmations, writing morning notes, personal prayer and scriptures study, exercise and nutritionals. On my PM routine, I make a plan for the next day, have personal prayer, meditation, visualization and affirmations. I end my day filling my brain with the positive affirmations. It is a great way to relax and have a more peaceful sleep.

Of course, there is a lot mixed in with reading bedtime stories, tucking kids in, etc. Generally, my personal lists are just things that I do on my own. It doesn't work out perfectly every single day, but as I've said before, it is about progress, not perfection. If I take the time to book-end my days by nourishing my body, heart, mind and soul, I know that if the rest of my day ends up getting crazy, I've at least done the essentials.

Divide Your Days

I like to categorize my days. There are so many things that need to be done in a week that when I divide up my tasks into specific days, it just feels more organized in my brain. I know that everything will get done, and it helps reduce stress. We all have many demands on our time, but there are certain things that need to be taken care of or our lives can begin to fall into chaos. I've divided my days into specific categories that I've listed below:

Monday – Cleaning / Laundry / Meal Prep Day
Tuesday – Errand Day (Health Coaching - Clients)
Wednesday – Desk Day (paperwork, correspondence, letters, blog, etc.)
Thursday – Project Day (Health Coaching - Clients)
Friday – Field Trip / Project Day

There is a lot of freedom here, and I don't always follow it perfectly, but it is a framework for getting the things done that I need. I love to have Mondays as my catch up day from the weekend. It starts my week out right when everything is back in order and when my meals are prepared for the week.

My project days are things that I am personally working on. I might be de-cluttering my home, putting scrapbooks together, doing business or working on my mentoring program. I have the flexibility within my schedule to meet the demands and needs of my family and myself.

Field trip days are activities that I plan with my little girls. We go to the zoo, park, museum, movie, visit grandparents, etc.

I found a great idea for summer planning from the website, *PowerofMoms.com* - a summer schedule for kids. We've done this for the past few years, and it provided a great framework for some order during the summer months and gave the kids something to look forward to.

Monday – Make it Monday (craft or baking project)
Tuesday – Take a field trip Tuesday
Wednesday – Wet Wednesday (this was our swimming day)
Thursday – Thankful Thursday (we tried to do some act of service for someone)
Friday – Friends Friday (this was the day designated for play-day for friends)

I have found that when I put this type of structure to my weekly schedule, I am able to keep up on my busy life as well as make sure the essential things are getting done and that I'm spending the quality time I want with my family.

Menu Planning and Shopping Lists

I've done menu planning and grocery lists for probably fifteen years. It has really simplified the frustration that comes with trying to figure out what to feed your family last minute. Over the last few years, I've revamped my menus to healthier, low-glycemic meals. My goal has been to really transform the way I eat and feed my family. Over the years, I haven't always been the best example of healthy eating. I know that I want to be healthy and vibrant and share that message with my family and others. I have four weeks of menus planned, and then I have a shopping list to go with each corresponding week of meals. This way, I don't have to spend time every week figuring out meals and making a new shopping list. I can just grab my list for that particular week and be out the door in no time.

I use one day per week to prepare my meals in advance so they literally take just minutes putting them together (this system is explained in the *Low-Glycemic Meals in Minutes* cookbook). Mondays are my cleaning, laundry and meal prep days. I cut up my veggies and cook my meats and put items in baggies. This really helps to simplify the mealtime preparation.

I have put together a 28-day program to Nourish Your Body and Rejuvenate Your Life. It includes all of my meal plans and shopping lists along with a whole lot more in nutritional information, videos and conference calls and other healthy goodies! You can learn more about my programs by going to StacyHarmer.com and contacting me.

Supportive Activity in Setting up Systems & Structure:

Create SYSTEMS – **S**ave **Y**our **S**elf **T**ime, **E**nergy and **M**oney

Create your AM and PM routines - Learn to book-end your days

AM	PM

Chapter 9

Branches: Discovering Your Purpose and Passion

T he branches on the tree represent finding your purpose and passion. It is this step that really begins to be fun and make life exciting. Finding and living our purpose will not be easy. It takes motivation and hard work. You will be uncomfortable. But as long as you always choose growth over comfort, you are on the right path to finding your purpose.

What are your strengths?

I'd like to share some questions that I've found helpful. What are your strengths? Sometimes it is easier for others to help identify our strengths for us. What do people say that you are good at? If you don't know, ask some family members or close friends to help identify what your strengths are and make a list.

What do you love to do?

Next, what is it that you love to do more than anything? There are certain things that we feel passionate about and other things that are of absolutely no interest to us. People rarely excel at tasks they don't enjoy doing or feel passionate about. One of the key indicators of this is level of enthusiasm. What do you do for sheer enjoyment? When we do what we are wired to love to do, you get good at it. Passion drives perfection. If you don't care about something, it is unlikely that you will excel at it. I've discovered that one of my passions is connecting, encouraging and supporting others. I was a cheerleader growing up for seven years through jr. high, high school and college. I loved expressing my energy and enthusiasm to support our teams. I've discovered that through coaching and personal mentoring, I am using these same passions to help people in their own personal lives, and it has brought me so much joy!

What are your natural abilities?

Everyone is born with specific, natural gifts and abilities. Being a mother of seven children, I can attest that children come out of the womb with different strengths and abilities. I have one son who has always been so curious and thinks deeply. I saw these strengths of his at a very young age, as he would analyze almost anything he could think about. I have a daughter who was always writing and leaving love notes wherever she would go. Her gift was to help others feel love. I have another son who can quote from almost any funny show he has ever seen. He continually makes everyone around him laugh and can raise the energy of a room very quickly. I have another son who loves and adores children. Even as a young child, he would always ask to hold or play with other babies or children. These are gifts that these children were born with.

When we use our natural gifts and abilities in our lives, we are using our God-given talents to bless others. It is important to recognize these gifts and tap into the power they have to bless and change lives.

What is your personality?

Next, take a look at your personality. We are each so unique! There are introverts and extroverts, people who love routine and those who love variety. There are thinkers and feelers. Some people like to work alone while others are energized by people. There are detailed oriented people and others who are visionaries. There is no right or wrong personality. Our personality will affect how and where we use our gifts and abilities.

What have been your primary life experiences?

Finally, our life experiences really mold our character and us. Think of your family, educational, spiritual and even painful experiences. It is usually the most painful experiences that we go through that will direct us to our purpose. I was comforted at the time of my loss by other mothers who had also lost children. I knew they knew what I was feeling and going through. My own journey with depression has brought a level of compassion to me for those who are struggling. My heart goes out to others who feel stuck in their lives and are unable to move forward or get out of their personal pit. My personal mission has been born out of my painful experiences and wanting to help others move forward with their lives. Aldous Huxley said, "Experience is not what happens to you. It is what you do with what happens to you." What will you do with what you've been through? Don't waste it. Use it to help others!

When we become clear on what we are meant to be doing in this world, life really becomes exciting. This is where the fun really kicks in, as time doesn't seem to matter any more. We do what we love and what we are good at. This is called living in your Zone of Genius. In his book, *The Big Leap*, Gay Hendricks identifies several different zones from incompetence, competence, excellence and genius. If we can move up the scale to find what really lights our fire and what we excel at, and what we would do whether we were paid or not, then we have truly found our genius and a gift to be shared with the world.

Supportive Activity in Discovering your Purpose and Passion:

1. What are your Strengths?

2. What do you Love to do?

3. What are your Natural Abilities?

4. What is your Personality Type?

5. What have been your meaningful or challenging Life Experiences?

Chapter 10

Fruit: Sharing Your Gifts

In the analogy of the tree, when our roots are being properly nourished, then the law of the harvest says we will produce fruit. There is a germination time period where it takes time for our roots to grow deep before the fruit is produced. Be patient with yourself if you are at the stage of deepening your roots. It will be worth the effort you expend in nourishing your body, heart, mind and soul. It is an ongoing, daily charge. Once fruit is being produced in our lives, it is our responsibility to share with others. Fruit on a tree that is not shared becomes ripe, then overripe and eventually drops to the ground. It is just a matter of time before the fruit will rot and make a mess. If we are not giving of our fruit, talents and gifts to others, we are limiting our positive influence, as well as probably making a mess in our own lives.

You were put on this earth to make a contribution. You weren't created just to consume resources and take up space. You were designed perfectly to make a difference with your life. This is not a section on how to "get" the most out of life, but how to "add" the most to this life on earth. We grow in order to give back. It is not enough to keep learning more and more. We must act and share what we know.

I love the quote, "Impression without expression causes depression." We are all meant to express ourselves. Our gifts and talents will vary a great deal. It may be a great work of art, a beautiful piece of music, or an ability to be a true friend and have a listening ear. One may be a teacher, an actor, a scientist or an inspirational speaker or leader. We will find joy and meaning as long as we are giving of our talents and ourselves to bless the lives of others. The comparison between the Sea of Galilee and the Dead Sea is still true. Galilee is a lake full of life because it takes in water but it also gives out. In contrast, nothing lives in the Dead Sea because with no outflow the lake has stagnated. The same is true with our lives. We must constantly be looking for ways to give back.

Conclusion and Summary

You are Meant to Succeed

Having gone through an extremely difficult and challenging time in my life, my heart goes out to others who are struggling. We are not put on this earth to fail. My heart breaks when I hear of others who take their own lives because of despair and hopelessness. I was lucky to get the help that I needed at a very low point in my life. That is why I can't keep quiet but must share the tools and steps that helped me overcome clinical depression and rebuild myself to have a whole, healthy, happy and vibrant life.

Of course we will have the ups and downs that come with being human. But once we understand what it takes to quickly flip things around and stay in a good place, there is no need to despair. Even with all of the tools I share, there is nothing that is more valuable than simply surrendering to God and allowing His power to heal lives. I do believe that He is the source of all healing but has given us tools, mentors and experiences to help us along this journey.

Be the hero of your own story! Each of us is writing our own story. It's not over until it's over, and we have the ability at any moment to change the direction of our lives if we have enough desire and determination. There will be adversity along the way. Adversity teaches us things we could not learn otherwise and accelerates that learning. I don't think anyone in their right mind would ask for challenges, trial or adversity. But once we go through these refining experiences and healing takes place, we can actually come to a place of gratitude for the lessons that we have learned along the journey. We can have gratitude for the person we have become through the experiences and see with new eyes in a way that we couldn't before.

We can appreciate the positive character traits we've developed through our challenges.

I have young daughters who love to read or watch fairy tales. There is always a hero or heroine who has to overcome adversity. In the movie *Frozen*, Elsa had to learn to control her personal powers by using love to bring about goodness and beauty versus the fear that brought about destruction. In *Beauty and the Beast*, Belle chose to give up her home and family to become captive to the beast in order to save her father. Adversity teaches us things that we could not learn otherwise and accelerates our learning curve. I'm continually inspired by others who have overcome their trials to live the lives they were destined to live.

One of my heroes in history is Abraham Lincoln. Did you know he was born into poverty and faced defeat throughout his life? He lost his mother at a young age and failed in business twice and then went bankrupt. His heart was broken when his sweetheart passed away after he was engaged to be married. He suffered a total nervous breakdown the following year and was in bed for six months. He lost eight elections before he became one of the greatest presidents in the history of our country. Even through the years of loss, heartache and trial, he was a champion and never gave up.

It doesn't matter how many times we fall. What matters is that we get up after each fall. Every experience teaches us a lesson, and individuals who have great success in life are often the ones who have the most failures but just refuse to quit.

The Chinese Bamboo Tree

One of my favorite parables on human growth and potential is that of the Chinese Bamboo Tree. Like any plant, it requires water, fertile soil, and sunshine to grow. Patience, faith and perseverance are all needed over the next five years when there is no visible growth above the soil. One might give up on such a plant if they had tenderly watered, fertilized and cared for this plant without seeing any results. But, something very important was going on deep under the soil during the first four years of life. The roots were growing deep within the ground, so when it was time for growth, the roots could support the rapid growth. Finally in the fifth year, the Chinese Bamboo Tree grows eighty feet in just six weeks! Had the tree not developed its strong root system and foundation, it could not have sustained its life as it grew.

The same is true for people. We must continually grow the roots in our own lives and build the character needed to sustain our growth and potential. It involves what has been shared in this book:

1) Nourishing our Bodies and developing good, healthy habits that include proper supplementation, low-glycemic whole and raw foods, exercise, adequate hydration and sleep.

2) Nourishing our Hearts by nurturing and developing healthy relationships, giving loving service and releasing negative emotions and replacing them with the positive.

3) Nourishing our Minds by studying great literature, people and ideas, and using the power of intention, affirmations and focus to create the life we desire.

4) Nourishing our Spirits by connecting to our Divine Source through prayer, meditation, scripture study, being in nature, journaling or whatever way that speaks to you.

As we continually nurture these basic areas in our lives, our roots will run deep to sustain the growth that will inevitably come. We must stay persistent and focused even if we don't see immediate results. Eventually the growth will come. And as we follow the remaining three steps by setting up systems and structure, discovering our purpose and passion and then ultimately sharing our gifts with others, we will find joy and meaning and truly live a vibrant life!

Vibrant Living Academy

A Community of Like-Minded Women

Stacy is the CEO and Founder of the Vibrant Living Academy – A Community of Like-Minded Women, where she has gathered women to help empower women. Our mission is to help heal lives. We are all about healing our bodies, hearts, minds, souls, relationships and finances – starting with the woman, who in turn helps heal her family, who in turn helps heal communities, who in turn helps heal the world!

We invite you to come join this fun and inspiring Academy and community of women by participating in mentoring, classes and workshops, an online website and membership forum worth tens of thousands of dollars in courses and mentoring such as: health and nutrition, emotional release work, finances, parenting, creating dream boards, affirmations, life vision, organization, nature study, preparedness, principles of creation, etc. Our purpose is also to provide a platform for women to further their outreach and share their purpose and passion.

In addition to the mentoring, we hold Vibrant Living Retreats, where you'll participate in interactive activities where you'll actually implement the material shared in this book. It is one thing to read it, it is another thing to get away in a beautiful setting and have a hands-on experience. When you participate in Vibrant Living Retreats, you'll be surrounded by other amazing like-minded people, have delicious, healthy whole and raw foods, walk away with nutritional knowledge, meal plans, shopping lists, skills to help you do emotional release work on yourself or your family, make a dream board, create affirmations and a Life Movie Script, meditate, go on a nature hike, create a beautiful handmade journal, do yoga, set up systems and routines for your home, discover your purpose and passion and share your talents, gifts and insights with others. Best of all, you'll connect with the hearts of some beautiful individuals who will move and change your life forever.

Something magical happens when a group gets together with the intention of connecting, learning, growing and desiring to make a difference in the world. You'll be inspired to create and live the life of your dreams, as well as assist others in their journey. To find more information about upcoming retreats and the Vibrant Living Academy and Community, visit StacyHarmer.com, VibrantLivingAcademy.org, or contact Stacy at Stacy@StacyHarmer.com.

About the Author

Stacy Harmer is a Certified Holistic Health Coach and a graduate from the Institute of Integrative Nutrition. She is a Raw Food Chef and Emotional Release Facilitator. She has her B.S. and M.S. degrees from Brigham Young University in Family Science and Education. She is a wife and mother of 7 children. She is passionate about helping others find joy and live vibrant lives. She works with individuals and groups alike in her Health Coaching Practice. She has online weight loss programs and teaches a variety of classes and workshops on health and healing. She is the CEO and Founder of the Vibrant Living Academy – A Community of Like-Minded Women, where she has gathered women to help empower and mentor each other on a variety of subjects focusing on healing bodies, hearts, minds, souls, relationships and finances.

She loves spending time with her family, traveling, being in nature, reading great books, playing the piano and doing anything creative. She loves to connect with the hearts and souls of others. Her path of healing has changed her life, and she loves to help others transform their lives by implementing the tools and techniques shared in this book.

Help Spread the Word

If the material in this book has spoken to you, or you find that you enjoy helping others in their lives, there is nothing better than teaching material to really absorb it! I'm looking for individuals who would like to certify to teach my 7 Steps to Vibrant Living Course or add the curriculum to their existing coaching or mentoring practice. Contact me at Stacy@StacyHarmer.com.

Speaking Engagements and Workshops

One of my passions is speaking and sharing these life-changing tools with others. I've witnessed firsthand how, by following this formula, you can truly transform your life. I've also had the privilege of assisting others on this journey, and their words speak for themselves. Some are shared in the introduction of this book. To contact me, please email: Stacy@StacyHarmer.com.

Made in the USA
San Bernardino, CA
22 April 2017